GW00759280

The Filby Files - Vol.2

CLASSIC KIT CARS

A COMPREHENSIVE BUYER'S GUIDE TO
EVERY KIT CAR PRODUCED BETWEEN 1953 & 1985

Written by Chris Rees

Edited by Peter Filby

BLUESTREAM BOOKS

The Filby Files - Vol.2

CLASSIC KIT CARS

A COMPREHENSIVE BUYER'S GUIDE TO EVERY KIT CAR PRODUCED BETWEEN 1953 & 1985

First published August 1997
© Bluestream Books

All rights reserved. No part of this publication may be reproduced or transmitted in any form or by any means, electronic or manual, including photocopying, recording or by any information storage or retrieval system, without prior permission in writing from the publisher.

ISBN: 1 901860 00 0

Published by
**Bluestream Books, 1 Howard Road, Reigate, Surrey RH2 7JE
Tel: 01737 222030 Fax: 01737 240185**

Graphics & repro by Apec Graphics, Reigate
Print by Grapevine, Sompting, W. Sussex

Acknowledgements

Huge thanks are due to all the people who have helped with this enormous project. I know Peter Filby gives himself a credit on the cover but he *has* spent months on the layout, picture research and editing sides and I pay full tribute to his passionate persistence and enthusiasm. A large debt is also owed to Ian Hyne for the supply of several pictures used in the book. Thanks also to Richard Heseltine, Gary Axon, Richard Oakes, Trevor Pyman, Dave Chivers, Bob Egginton, Pam Johns, Tim Dutton, the Gilbern Owners Club, John Jobber, Roger Wooley, the Mini-Marcos Owners Club, Alan Hatswell, Alan Arnold, Martin Vincent and Pen Roberts, plus everyone else whose name I have neglected to mention.

Foreword

By Peter Filby

I'VE BEEN THINKING OF PUBLISHING THIS BOOK FOR several years. There's never been a shortage of books on the most famous British cars such as the MG, Mini, Triumph, Bentley and Lotus, and there have been several titles covering specialist sports cars like the Marcos, TVR, Morgan, Panther and Caterham. But no nicely presented, professionally produced works on that much maligned breed, the kit car. So, to my mind at least, this has always represented a big gap on the book shelves covering British automotive history.

The Filby Files four-volume series aims to plug this gap in no uncertain terms. We start – oddly enough, I know – with Volume 2, but that's because it seemed logical to me that Volume 1 should cover cars belonging to an earlier period than those in Volume 2. And Volume 1 hasn't been written yet!

Whether the purists like it or not, the British kit car industry has employed a lot of fine engineering talent and produced a multitude of fascinating sports cars. Great creativity and innovation have always taken place in the industry's many small workshops and factories dotted around the country, and the results have always been intriguing, often absolutely inspiring: just look at the huge success of Marcos, Lotus, TVR and Caterham Cars, all of whom started out making kits.

Of course, kit cars have always had an extremely maddening and frustrating ability to span the enormous divide between brilliant and devastatingly awful. Some models are beautifully styled, superbly engineered, innovative and exhilarating to drive; others are pig ugly, bordering on dangerous and a nightmare to drive. That's something those of us who've worked with this fascinating industry have learned to live with. It's certainly taught us great patience and toleration.

Fabulous, capable, mediocre or disastrous, they're all in this book – at least, all those produced between 1953 and 1985. And lucky old me has personally driven a fair percentage of them, for both work and pleasure. I began my love affair – no, call it infatuation – with individual, strange and often bizarre motor cars around 1970 with a Unipower GT. Mid-engined, Mini Cooper 1275 'S' powered and with a 40" high coupé body over a spaceframe chassis, it was a highly entertaining and rewarding machine. A true classic kit car, nowadays very collectable and worth quite a lot of money.

Inexplicably, other than perhaps being broke, I soon went downhill to the lower mid-range of the kit car spectrum by swapping my Unipower for a Maya GT, then a Peel Viking Minisport. Then a Heron Europa, Trident Venturer, Magenta

LSR, Hustler 6-wheeler and so on, and so on. Somewhere in the midst of catching – and failing to resist – the kit car bug, I found myself in worryingly uncertain employment with the likes of a beach buggy manufacturer, Davrian Developments of Clapham, South-East London, and the Nova manufacturers up north in Accrington.

At the same time, I was trying to supplement my meagre or non-existent earnings with some free-lance writing – about kit cars, of course. After working for magazines like *Car, Auto Enthusiast, Motor* and *Autocar*, I soon became well known for my specialist knowledge and wide range of unlikely, not always useful, contacts. Some people even referred to me as 'the expert on kit cars'.

Whatever, I went on to write a regular column for *Hot Car* and finally to launch my own magazines, *Alternative Cars* and predictably enough, *Kit Car*.

Above: The Filby Maya GT ended up much modified with oblong headlamps and a deep spoiler. This, and its occasional unreliaility, landed it with the name Maya Maynot! Below: The editor's much loved Cooper 1275 'S' powered Unipower GT, inexplicably sold to make way for the Maya.

They succeeded almost instantly: there had always been an obvious demand for information about specialist cars, kit cars and anything else a bit odd-ball. To cut a long story short, this all led, one way or another, to my current publishing operations: *Which Kit?*, Britain's leading kit car monthly, the reputable *Which Kit? Guide* annual and a growing range of specialist car books. So, hopefully, I'm fairly well qualified to be the engine room, editor and publisher of *The Filby Files, Volume 2: Classic Kit Cars.*

As it happens, Chris Rees is absolutely the perfect man to write it, and what a terrific job he's done. We sort of hatched the original plan together, but Chris was the lucky man who got the job of penning the endless mini-histories and information panels that make up the bulk of the book. Is he quite brilliant, merely painstakingly meticulous or slightly off his trolley? All of them, I think, because he has certainly compiled and coerced into published history the ultimate reference work to every production and prototype kit car produced between 1953 and 1985, and it must have taken almost unimaginable patience and devotion.

Chris and I produced this book not only because we saw it would fill a big gap but also because we knew we would enjoy doing it. I can speak for both of us in saying that has certainly been the case. We hope you gain as much pleasure from reading it and using it as an informative reference work. But be warned: there are three more equally fascinating volumes to come in *The Filby Files* series – see page 129 for more information. We'll talk to you again very soon...

Introduction

BUYING A USED KIT CAR – THE VERY IDEA CAN send shudders down your back. Getting involved with *any* used car is a risky business, let alone a car which some often unknown amateur builder has built up from a box of parts.

But follow a few simple rules and you don't have to come unstuck. Indeed, buying a used kit can be an amazingly good idea. Firstly, you don't have to build the thing yourself – someone else has done it for you. Secondly, it will frequently cost you less to buy a full-spec built-up kit than it would to get just the kit alone from the manufacturer (people rarely make a profit out of building a kit car). Thirdly, you will be owning a slice of that rare pudding, the specialist car industry. Fourth, your choice expands to include cars which have long since been out of production.

The trouble is finding the right information about this diverse and surprising breed of cars. That's why *Classic Kit Cars* has been created.

This book is the first in a series of titles under the *Filby Files* brand name. Together, the complete set will provide a comprehensive overview of specialist and kit cars offered for sale in Great Britain. This is Volume 2 in the series, and covers all true kit cars sold in Britain from around 1953 up until 1985. Why 1985? Simply because we found that the number of kit model types split equally in the periods before and after that year. Thus the forthcoming Volume 4 in the series will cover the period 1985-97. Two further volumes will cover (a) the early specials era of the 1950s and early 1960s and (b) fully-built British specialist sports cars sold only in turn-key form.

Because kit cars are so diverse in scope and number, and because people all too often don't really know what they are buying when looking at second-hand examples, this book's main objective is to act as a useful, informative buyer's guide. Each

Eccentric Siva Edwardian Roadster has been out of production since 1974. Great fun potential but be careful over your purchase.

model is given a complete description and some qualitative comments about its good and bad points. We also include the current manufacturer's location if the car is still made.

We have also given guide prices for all the major kits. It must be stressed that these are *guide figures only* and not cast-in-stone values. Pricing used kit cars is more fraught with problems than other fields of the car industry because of the cavernous divide between the specifications of individual cars and the standards to which they have been built.

At the end of the day, as with anything else, a kit car is worth what someone is prepared to pay for it. But there is such a thing as a ball-park figure, which is what we have provided. See the separate section later in this introduction for a full explanation of our price guide figures.

For those utterly obscure kits of which only a tiny handful were made (sometimes only one), we have also included an A-Z section at the back of this book for all those oddities that you might just come across. So if someone has advertised a Graham Autos Dreambird, you know where to look to find out what the hell it is. As for values for these obscure cars, frankly your guess is as good as ours – do your own haggling!

GUIDELINES

There are some golden rules that are well worth considering when buying kit cars:

1 – Is the car what the vendor says it is?
This is often difficult to establish, especially where replicas are concerned. The difference in worth between a Cheetah Cobra and a Ram SC is huge, yet it is not unknown for a lesser replica to be described as a greater one. Look at the chassis plate and check with the manufacturer (if one still exists) or with an owners' club.

Early TVR Grantura from mid-1960s is an appreciating classic. Lots of help and advice available from an enthusiastic owner's club.

2 – If a car is described as 'almost complete', check that it can actually be finished.
Unbuildable kits sadly do exist. Our advice with these is to stick where possible with well known and *current* kits, so that you do actually stand a chance of completing it. This guide does not cover the grey area of which kits are more buildable than others, nor does it aim to offer prices for unfinished kits. At least with a fully finished kit, you are sure that it all goes together.

3 – Be aware if the car is no longer made.
You could have trouble fixing the car if it goes wrong or in replacing parts if it is involved in an accident. The body moulds may no longer exist.

Desirable models like this Turner Sports and Rochdale Olympic are occasionally found for sale in classic car magazines. Be quick though!

4 – Look in the right place to find your car.
The classified pages of *Which Kit?* magazine or other kit publications are the best source for kit cars. Owners advertising their wares here tend to be enthusiasts. Other publications worth trying are *Exchange & Mart* (which has a special kit car section), *Auto Trader*, classic car titles and local advertisement rags like *London's Loot*. There are now several kit car dealers and specialised marque dealers who are often worth checking out. In many cases, kit car manufacturers themselves have second-hand cars for sale (or know where to find them), and can offer extremely valuable advice, while owners' clubs frequently have a section in their newsletters for used members' cars.

5 – Accept that older kit cars will need overhauling or maybe rebuilding.
Just like classic cars, older kits will at some stage need restoring. Often this can pose problems because of parts supplies, or you may uncover all sorts of things which the original builder has done which you would like to change. In many cases, it may actually be easier and cheaper to build your

own kit car new from scratch. For these reasons, avoid basket cases, botch jobs and rough non-standard cars. Generally, glassfibre is easy to repair if damaged or crazed, but it's best left to the professionals. The same comment applies to painting glassfibre or aluminium.

6 – Join an owners' club.
Tremendous support (whether technical or psychological) is available from one of the many dedicated or non-dedicated/regional kit car clubs. As the proverb goes, a problem shared...

7 – Safety first.
If you're at all unsure about any safety-related item, walk away. In particular, look at safety belt anchorages, sharp edges, welded joints, mounting points for suspension, engine, seats, steering, etc. Also get acquainted with Construction & Use regulations so that you can spot potential problems of legality with lighting, tyre width, glass and so on.

8 – Follow the basic rules about car buying.
In other words, be thorough, be patient, be sure of yourself. For more information about what specifically to look for when you're inspecting a car, read Peter Wallage's article in *Which Kit?* magazine of June 1994. Photocopies of the article are available if you ring the magazine on 01737 225565 and order by credit card.

STAR RATINGS
Each of the main guide entries has a 'star rating' based on the soundness of the general concept, quality of design and quality of manufacture. Bear in mind that individual examples of kit cars can vary wildly, and therefore that the star ratings are intended as a guide only and will frequently be controversial – and that's partly the point. Five stars is the top end, one star is the dustbin end.

GUIDE PRICES
We have aimed to give three guide prices to second-hand values where possible, as follows:

A – Demonstrably well-built cars, probably with plenty of documentation, a high level of specification and needing no work at all. Typically will have many reconditioned/new parts or been subject to a recent, high quality restoration to original speciification. Concours and exceptionally good cars may fetch more.

B – Sound, useable examples which should be presentable. Some cosmetic attention will probably be required, and perhaps a few small mechanical

Alto

☆☆

Prod Years: 1983-84
Prod Numbers: Very few
For: Similar exotic looks to Avante, if you like the appearance but want a mid-engine an Alfachassis one might suit, cheap
Against: Not very sophisticated chassis, build quality poor, Beetle engined ones not very exotic
Verdict: Good looking Avante clone
Price Guide
A £3000   **B** £1700   **C** £800
Current Maker: None

There is little room for debate that the Alto was a pretty close rip-off of the Avante (see page 15). It was made by a company called Peerhouse Cars based in Surrey, and had close links with Sandwood Automotive, who offered their mid-engined Alfachassis under the GRP shell. Other alternatives were a VW Beetle floor-pan and VW Golf power. A full kit including the Alfachassis cost a pretty hefty £3500 plus VAT (at a time when the complete Avante kit cost £2550), so this venture was short-lived. However, a revival was executed in 1988 by Cardo Engineering – it was unsuccessful.

Anglebug

☆☆

Prod Years: 1971-72
Prod Numbers: A few
For: It's a buggy with a front-mounted engine, so handling should be reasonable and roadholding acceptable
Against: Looks bloody stupid (check out the Anglia headlamps), not exactly exotic, lousy performance
Verdict: World's first and only Ford Anglia based buggy - perfect for Southend in 1971...
Price Guide
A £1000   **B** £700   **C** £400
Current Maker: None

Beach buggies were born in the USA - or more accurately, dune buggies were born in the USA. Transplanted to Britain, they made much less sense. One of the most idiotic of all was the Anglebug, which eschewed Beetle power for the exotic alternative of Ford Anglia basis. This had the effect of making the usual buggy styling look ridiculous (the front end was much higher than most buggies to accommodate the Anglia engine), while the 997cc engine was hardly spine-tingling in its coolness. At least one example had two sets of wheels on one axle.

Apal Buggy

☆☆

Prod Years: 1971-92
Prod Numbers: Quite a few
For: It looks a little different from most buggies
Against: Usual buggy demerits, plus you won't be able to replace the original bodywork if it's damaged
Verdict: Certainly not Apal-ing, but a paltry justification
Price Guide
A £1200   **B** £900   **C** £500
Current Maker: None

Belgium's leading alternative car manufacturer also made buggies, dating back to the great fun car boom of the early 1970s. A British firm called Cartune acquired the licence to import, then manufacture, the Apal in 1971. *Custom Car* magazine said: "stylistically not the greatest thing since smokey bacon crisps" but at least it looked different from all the GP buggy clones over here. Lightspeed Panels (makers of the Magenta) took it over in 1972 and made a few more. Following a spell with GT Mouldings, last known owners of the moulds were a company called Country Volks.

Apal Speedster

☆☆☆☆☆

Prod Years: 1981-date (in Belgium)
Prod Numbers: Approx 500
For: Extremely high quality, high degree of authenticity, the longest-running Speedster replica in history
Against: Liable to be expensive, spares have to be imported from Belgium
Verdict: Thoroughly credible and high-quality Speedster replica
Price Guide
A £7500   **B** £4500   **C** £2400
Current Maker: Apal, Belgium

Belgian Porsche 356 Speedster replica by the famous firm Apal, which took over the licence to produce this replica from Italo-American pioneer Intermeccanica. First sold (briefly) in the UK by Dutton as the Starborne, then TPC from 1984, when it was outrageously expensive, then (from 1992) by Speedsters and latterly The Classic Carriage Company. Shortened VW floorpan, strengthening steel tube perimeter frame, non-MacPherson strut Beetle parts. Very high quality and accuracy, though rare here because of marked-up retail prices; that could make one a real bargain, however. No longer imported.

Arkley S/SS

☆☆☆☆☆

Morgan dealers John Britten Garages of Arkley, Herts, created this one. When Midgets were ten-a-penny, this was an extremely popular way of looking different for not much cash. Just remove front and rear bodywork and replace it with new glass-fibre panels with a fun car/traditional cross-over flavour and - *voila!* - it doesn't look anything like an MG. Earliest ones had cut-away doors, too, and there was a simple S version with slimmer wheels, though the fat-arch SS version is by far the more numerous. These days, Midgets are more likely to be restored than converted to Arkleys, but they are well known within MG clubs.

Prod Years: 1970-date
Prod Numbers: Approx 900
For: Extreme practicality thanks to MG Midget basis (including a decent hood), and most of it doesn't rust
Against: Still some ancient metalwork there, though
Verdict: If you're into flares and plat-forms, you'll love the Arkley
Price Guide
A £2500   B £1500   C £1000
Current Maker: Peter May Engineering, Halesowen

ASD Minim

☆☆☆☆☆

"A latterday Austin-Healey Sprite" was how the Minim's creator, Bob Egginton, described his little mid-engined roadster. That's pretty accurate: it was a low cost, simple, fun two-seater which also hap-pened to be very good at going round corners. Steel backbone chassis, bolt-on glassfibre body, half-doors, Mini wind-screen, Mini engine mounted amidships still within its subframe. The target market was young people and female drivers, but very few were sold. Egginton's ASD is per-haps better known for its race car prepa-ration, putting projects like the Minim on the back-burner.

Prod Years: 1984-date
Prod Numbers: 6
For: Sound engineering, low centre of gravity and mid engine means excellent cornering, light weight, practicality
Against: Too-tall Mini screen makes it look a bit funny
Verdict: If you find one for sale, it could make a great little sports car
Price Guide
A £3000   B £2200   C £1500
Current Maker: Automotive Systems Development, Leeds, Kent

Ashley 1172

☆☆☆☆☆

Ashley Laminates was one of the early glassfibre shell makers, born in 1954. Its first 'proper' kit was the 1172. This was commonly sold as a basic shell for a modi-fied Ford E93A chassis in open or hardtop forms (the latter sometimes known as the GT), and short wheelbase (90in) two-seater or long wheelbase (94in) four-seater forms. From 1958 you could opt for Ashley's own Regent ladder chassis (coil spring suspension as opposed to leaves). Engines options included Ford sidevalve, BMC A-series, 100E/105E and MGA/MGB. An Ashley body shell formed the basis of the Reliant Sabre.

Prod Years: 1958-62
Prod Numbers: Several hundred
For: Far more handsome than most Ford based specials of the era, and better made, simple mechanically, some classic credentials
Against: Usual lack of sophistication, likely to be an asthmatic performer
Verdict: A cut above the usual Ford specials stuff
Price Guide
A £3000   B £1800   C £1000
Current Maker: None

Ashley Sportiva

☆☆☆☆☆

Unlike the 1172, the 1961 Sportiva was offered exclusively as a complete car in component form. Visually it differed in having a shorter nose with exposed head-lamps and a squarish grille, aesthetically not as pleasing as earlier Ashleys. In other respects it was very similar to the 1172, and was offered in open and closed forms and with two or four seats. But it also retained many of the 1172's shortcomings. Shortly after the company moved from Loughton to Harlow, the demand for such specials evaporated, and Ashley's GRP hardtop business could not support its continued existence on the price lists.

Prod Years: 1961-62
Prod Numbers: A few
For: Still quite pretty, flanged edges betray some sense of sophistication
Against: Less handsome than earlier Ashleys, and no less crude
Verdict: A marginally more refined and desirable 1172
Price Guide
A £3000   B £1800   C £1000
Current Maker: None

Atlantis

☆☆☆☆☆☆

Prod Years: 1982-86
Prod Numbers: Approx 15
For: Imposing looks, fine quality of construction, lots of luxury, refined road manners, aura of quality, four-seat practicality
Against: Fixed-head is rather cramped inside despite huge overall length
Verdict: A wonderful slice of *la belle epoque* - highly recommended
Price Guide
A £12,000   **B** £8000   **C** £5500
Current Maker: None

This fabulous 1930s style touring car was created in 1982 by Michael Booth, initially in complete form at prices from £39,000, but soon after as an up-market kit as well. The Figoni inspired, moulded glassfibre bodywork was initially sold as a fixed-head with four seats, but from 1985 a full drophead coupe was also available. Mechanicals derived from the Jaguar XJ, but at least one Atlantis was fitted with a big block V8. Though the Atlantis was theoretically available through the 1980s, the last one was built in 1986. Amazingly, one example competed with some success in the Kit Car Racing series.

Autotune Aristocat

☆☆☆☆☆

Prod Years: 1984-date
Prod Numbers: Approx 300
For: Very tough chassis and body construction, race proven, Jaguar parts give fine performance and ride
Against: Complex, not an accurate XK140 replica
Verdict: Solid, rapid transport for the would-be replica racer
Price Guide
A £10,000   **B** £6000   **C** £3500
Current Maker: Autotune, Rishton, Lancs

To call this a replica would not be accurate: although the Aristocat clearly evokes the style and presence of the Jaguar XK140, it is significantly wider than the original Jag, a fact which can be readily deduced from the wide-set radiator grille (although a Fixed Head model from 1991 returned to the original dimensions – see Volume 4). The reason was the width of the donor Jag XJ6 subframes and axles. Anthony Taylor conceived it for historic replica racing, with a huge space frame chassis and Jaguar mechanicals all round. Probably better to avoid part-built kits.

Avante

☆☆☆

Prod Years: 1982-86
Prod Numbers: Approx 30 (inc +2)
For: Fairly exotic and professional looks, simplicity of VW donor parts, budget buy
Against: Crude in many areas and build quality not up to much, phutt-phutting phlat-four Beetle engine is a real downer for the image
Verdict: More original alternative to a Nova or Eagle SS
Price Guide
A £3500   **B** £2000   **C** £1200
Current Maker: None

Just when most people were writing off the idea of Beetle-based exotikits, the Avante cropped up. Interesting and attractive Melvyn Kay styling made it stand out and found favour with quite a few customers. Always a Beetle floorpan, though it could be had with water-cooled 'fours' like the Golf GTI. Mk2 versions gained more space in the engine bay and sharper front-end treatment. Two-seater and 2+2 versions were on offer. Two rip-offs were made in the early days: the Peerhouse Alto (see page 13) and the Scorpione. Conventional doors and winding windows are benefits.

Avante +2

☆☆☆

Prod Years: 1983-86
Prod Numbers: see Avante
For: More mature shape than Avante, extra two seats and better engine access, cheap to run
Against: Ugly 'Iron girder' bumpers, VW Beetle basis, poor performance
Verdict: Forgotten Vee Dub exotic
Price Guide
A £2500   **B** £1500   **C** £800
Current Maker: None

The second generation Avante was in several respects a quite different beast to the first car. It was eight inches longer, six inches higher and had better ground clearance. The headlamps and arches were bigger, there were new rear side windows, much bigger opening engine lid, detachable sills and new separate bumpers. The body support frame was strengthened, though the VW Beetle floorpan remained. Most important change was a lot more space inside, allowing the addition of two extra seats in the back. These 2+2 Avante kits were now more expensive (up to £2250 plus VAT).

Baja GT/Sahara

If you are bored of the usual Meyers Manx/GP buggy styling, why not seek out a Baja GT? This was a heavily restyled GP Buggy on a shortened VW floorpan, with stylised curves and a fixed roll-over/targa bar, which made it much more practical than most of the dune prunes. Manufactured by Speed Buggys (sic) of Chichester before Jago Automotive and then Audy Marine took it over as a very marginal product. Then, in 1982, it came to rest with the Godfather of buggies James Hale, proprietor of GT Mouldings. He created a long wheelbase version which he called the Sahara.

Prod Years: 1971-date
Prod Numbers: Approx 35
For: Great if you like curvy bits, stands out from the buggy crowd
Against: 'GT' tag is a little optimistic, it's still basically a GP buggy underneath, not exactly pretty
Verdict: It may have been a novelty in 1971, but it's certainly not now
Price Guide
A £1200   **B** £800   **C** £500
Current Maker: GT Mouldings, Brighton

Beaujangle Can-Am

The first product of Beaujangle Enterprises, Manchester, was a cheap T-bucket in 1971. The Can-Am arrived in 1972, based on an American kit car design, supposedly inspired by US Can-Am racers. Basis was a VW floorpan shortened by 5in with suspension modifications to improve handling. The doorless GRP body stood only 36in high and the whole thing weighed just 11cwt. Options included a roll-over bar and gullwing hardtop, neither improving the car's fortunes. Amazingly, this buggy era drop-out was revived by Lemazone in 1985, but it is believed that no more kits were actually supplied.

Prod Years: 1972-73/1985
Prod Numbers: 6
For: Squashed pancake styling is dramatic if nothing else, Beetle mechanicals are simple, gullwing hardtop is novel
Against: Flat screen and Beetle headlamps look awkward, it's all a mite impractical and unconvincing
Verdict: Perfect for VW Beetle/soul brother cross-over fans
Price Guide
A £1800   **B** £1000   **C** £500
Current Maker: None

Beaver

Richard Oakes was named as the man who styled this estate kit car, but he says the design was finished off by someone else and it never looked right. That much is apparent: the Beaver was thoroughly uninspiring to look at, a factor dictated perhaps by the Ford Escort windscreen and doors. Conceived as a Dutton Sierra competitor, the Beaver was made by Kit Cars International of Barnsley and, when revived in 1991, by Beaver Coach Works. It did at least feature a highly professional standard of glassfibre moulding. As many parts as possible were taken from the Ford Escort and placed in a steel chassis.

Prod Years: 1984-85/1991-92
Prod Numbers: Few
For: High quality of construction, practicality, it blends into the background in a most un-kit car-like way
Against: Dull as dishwater
Verdict: Like an Escort Mk2 estate, except that it doesn't rust as much
Price Guide
A £1500   **B** £1000   **C** £500
Current Maker: None

Bedouin

Citroen realised the potential of its 2CV chassis for utilitarian applications when it produced the Mehari from 1968. The Bedouin was an enclosed, British built equivalent. It used an unmodified Citroen 2CV/Dyane/Ami floorpan to which was bolted an estate-type body of startlingly uncompromising boxiness. Early bodies were made in plywood, but later ones increased the content of glassfibre. They also made a camper conversion to which you could attach a voluminous tent. You might also see this car with a badge reading Ranger or Snowdonia, names used for the alternative camping versions.

Prod Years: 1985-87
Prod Numbers: Approx 20
For: Practicality, simple and reliable mechanicals, eminently durable/repairable and rust-free bodywork, undoubted fun factor
Against: Severely underpowered, 2CV floorpan prone to corrosion, very stark nature
Verdict: Worthy and rare utilitarian with surprising talent
Price Guide
A £2000   **B** £1400   **C** £900
Current Maker: None

Bilmar Buccaneer

Prod Years: 1971-72
Prod Numbers: 11
For: Lotus Seven type styling and lay-out (though slightly more practical), curiosity value
Against: Looks a bit weird from some angles, Spitfire engine does not promise much
Verdict: Highly obscure kit car - tell us if you find one!
Price Guide
A £4000   **B** £2000   **C** £1000
Current Maker: None

Not much is known about the Buccaneer, built by a concern known as Bilmar in Portland, Dorset, from 1971. Alongside the Dutton, it was a very early attempt to cash in on the continuing success of the Lotus Seven. The front wings and nose-cone were virtually identical, though it was over a foot wider than the Seven, sported very large headlamps and did not look happy from all angles. It featured alloy body panels over a space frame chassis, and the standard spec was a Triumph Spitfire engine with matching gearbox and front suspension, plus Ford Corsair rear axle. It didn't last long.

Biota

Prod Years: 1969-76
Prod Numbers: Approx 36
For: Race-proven chassis, superior handling, extremely light weight, Mini mechanicals are a known quantity
Against: Not very refined, dashed ugly from the rear
Verdict: Well worth investigating if you find one - a lot of fun and surprising ability awaits
Price Guide
A £1500   **B** £1000   **C** £500
Current Maker: None

Surprisingly able Mini-based sports car with a proper space frame chassis, Mini front subframe and Mini trailing arm/coil sprung rear. Unusual doorless GRP body incorporated a distinctive roll-over bar and a large bonnet bulge to accommodate the tall Mini engine. Bizarre facia-mounted gear lever and combined brake/accelerator 'stirrup', rare optional gullwing hardtop. Only 8cwt heavy, so real performance available - regular success at hillclimbs bolstered Yorkshire manufacturers Houghton Coldwell. Improved 1972 Mk2 version has De Dion rear suspension, hinged bonnet and bigger cockpit.

Boler T-Bone

Prod Years: 1971-74
Prod Numbers: Approx 30
For: Four people can sit in one
Against: They'll all want to get out straight away
Verdict: Surely the naffest pile of old cack ever invented
Price Guide
Don't even consider it
Current Maker: None

We've left the grey area of street rods out of this guide, but Lancastrian David Boler's T-Bone was less of a 'bucket' shell than most, and more of a true kit car. Early ones had Riley 1.5 running gear, though some got Ford rear axles. The majority were MGB based, and there was even a long wheelbase Jaguar XJ based option (only four of these were made). Hell, there was even one fitted with an Austin 3-litre engine. The main bodywork was all metal, while the wings and hardtop were glassfibre. Bernard Manning drove one and that just about sums up the Boler's utter lack of any redeeming features.

Bonito

Prod Years: 1981-87
Prod Numbers: Quite a few
For: Reasonable looks, usually good quality moulding, Seraph chassis is preferable to VW floorpan
Against: VW engines, never really very sophisticated
Verdict: Only mildly engaging sports coupe, a bit of a 'yesterday's car'
Price Guide
A £3500   **B** £2000   **C** £1000
Current Maker: None

The Bonito began life in the 1970s in Germany, where leading kit car makers Fiberfab created this Ford GT40-ish coupe on a VW Beetle floorpan. A British company called ACM imported it from 1981, then made it over here, still with such Teutonisms as a Ford Taunus P6 windscreen and Opel Rekord rear screen. Taken over by AED in 1983, who developed a convertible version, then passed it on to Seraph Cars in 1985 - who at last made a proper backbone chassis for it, based around Cortina front suspension, live rear axle and front-mounted Ford 4-cylinder and V6 engines (see Volume 4).

BRA 289

⭐⭐⭐⭐☆

Restoration experts John Berry and Peter Ibbotson formed Beribo Replica Automobiles and began work on their Cobra replica as early as 1976, though it was moulded from an original 289 narrow-arch model. The first examples incorporated some design mods (like a front spoiler, aero screens, squared wheel arches and bigger interior), but a demand for accurate replicas was quickly identified and virtually all BRAs look very authentic. MGB mechanicals in a steel multi-tube chassis, double wishbone front suspension, leaf sprung live axle rear. V8 version also offered from 1982.

Prod Years: 1981-date
Prod Numbers: Approx 250
For: Very high quality of design and manufacture, built up to a quality, better performance than an MGB
Against: MGB mechanicals not conducive to authenticity
Verdict: The original 289 replica and it is still the best
Price Guide
A £14,000   **B** £9000   **C** £4500
Current Maker: Tyler Industrial Mouldings, Hoo, Kent

BRA 427

⭐⭐⭐⭐☆

When BRA cottoned on to the fact that Cobra replica builders preferred the later-style 427 Cobra, it decided to supplement its existing 289 with a new 427 replica. True to the themes prevalent in this area, it boasted Jaguar suspension in a platform chassis designed by Gerry Hawkridge (later of Transformer Cars). Rover V8 engines were the recommended power units, though American V8s were possible. After a disappointingly poor sales performance (other makers had already stolen a march on the 427 market), the project was eventually sold to a German firm.

Prod Years: 1984-87
Prod Numbers: Very few
For: Usual BRA high quality manufacture, competent chassis engineering, V8 power options
Against: Finding one might be hard
Verdict: If you do find one, it will have been worth the effort
Price Guide
A £15,000   **B** £11,000   **C** £8000
Current Maker: None

BRA J-Type

⭐⭐⭐⭐☆

Nick Green's NG Cars had been doing rather well with its pretty 1930s style roadsters, and Doncaster based BRA tackled them head-on with the J-Type in 1984. This was a classic style two-seater inspired by the 1930s MG Midget, with a chassis designed to accept MGB suspension and a choice of MG or Ford engines. The quality was beyond reproach but the price was too high for it to make much impact. The J-Type had cycle front wings, in contrast to its later sister-model, the full-fendered P-Type. The project came up for sale in 1992 and was eventually bought in 1995 by enthusiast Rodney Rushton.

Prod Years: 1984-92/1995-date
Prod Numbers: Approx 60 (inc P-Type)
For: Well conceived chassis, very high quality execution, unlike most NGs you get proper doors
Against: Not easy to find one
Verdict: Superior traditional tourer - highly recommended
Price Guide
A £6500   **B** £4200   **C** £2200
Current Maker: Rodney Rushton, Cheriton Bishop, Exeter

BRA P-Type

⭐⭐⭐⭐☆

While the classically elegant J-Type continued to be offered in its original cycle-wing format, BRA developed the even prettier P-Type as a sister model. Its only distinguishing feature was a set of elegant flowing wings, which made it look more like a post-war MG, while the J-Type could be mistaken for a pre-war one. In all other respects, the P-Type shared its sister's MGB based specification entirely. When revived by Rodney Rushton's operation in 1995, it was just known as the P-Type and is still available new in kit form with J-Type cycle wings or the prettier flowing P-Type fenders.

Prod Years: 1985-92/1995-date
Prod Numbers: See J-Type
For: Same excellent engineering as the J-Type but prettier thanks to the full wing treatment, four seats
Against: Inherent impracticalities of the breed, they are rare
Verdict: Very near the top of the trad roadster ladder
Price Guide
A £6500   **B** £4200   **C** £2200
Current Maker: Rodney Rushton, Cheriton Bishop, Exeter

Bugle

☆☆☆☆

Prod Years: 1970-72/1979-85
Prod Numbers: Around 850
For: Novel appearance, many had lockable boots, 850 people can't all have been wrong, surely?
Against: Usual buggy crudities, it's not made any more
Verdict: This buggy's clarion call is fading rapidly
Price Guide
A £2000   **B** £1000   **C** £500
Current Maker: None

Mildly original buggy produced by Roland Sharman's London company, Lotusmere. Styling inspired by the American Bugetta: sloped headlamps, side panelling and (optional) reverse-angle roll-over bar/rear screen. Shortened VW floorpan, naturally, though a stretched Plus 2 version (from 1971) fitted an umodified Beetle chassis (but only 20 of these were ever made). Project was a casualty of the buggy bubble bursting, but Chris Watson's Yorkshire-based garage CW Autos revived it in 1979, though with few takers. The moulds ended up, like most forlorn British buggies, at GT Mouldings of Brighton.

Bullock

☆☆

Prod Years: 1972-73
Prod Numbers: About 35
For: You're not in danger of being ignored
Against: But you are in danger of being seriously laughed at
Verdict: Ugly by name, ugly by nature: so dreadful it might actually be cool - who knows?
Price Guide
A £1000   **B** £600   **C** £300
Current Maker: None

In a strange way, this car's name seems to suit the ham-fistedly ugly lines. The man responsible was one Andrew Ainsworth of Shepperton. His singularly inelegant two-seater consisted of a glassfibre body mounted on a pre-drilled box section chassis for Ford Anglia parts (though any Ford engine could be fitted). First produced as the Bullock B1, the follow-up B2 employed Triumph Herald front suspension, which obviated the need for the bulbous headlamp pods which sprouted from the B1's one-piece bonnet. Something of a mayfly, but amazingly about three dozen were sold, which says a lot about 1970s kit cars.

Burlington SS

☆☆☆☆

Prod Years: 1980-86
Prod Numbers: Around 200
For: Classically attractive Morgan-style lines, likely to be cheap
Against: Unlikely to fool anyone, Triumph mechanicals not very wonderful, check woodwork for rot
Verdict: Early but rather crude Morgan lookalike
Price Guide
A £2500   **B** £1200   **C** £500
Current Maker: None

Haydn Davis built his traditional style car in a workshop in Kenilworth around the wings and nose cone of the Morgan (which the customer had to buy separately). A Triumph Herald/Vitesse backbone chassis sat underneath it, though the engine was moved rearwards and the suspension modified. Metal-and-GRP-jointed plywood main body frame clad in aluminium looked very Morganesque (except for the lack of doors). Purpose-designed chassis available from 1982 for Marina/MGB/Ford Escort drive trains. The project was sold off to a company called Dorian in 1986 and made for two more years (see Volume 4).

Burlington Arrow

☆☆☆☆

Prod Years: 1982-92
Prod Numbers: Hundreds of plans sets were sold
For: Cheap route into '30s style motoring, good looks
Against: Crude, home-built bodies vary widely in quality, check Triumph chassis for rust, special chassis for sound welding
Verdict: Bargain basement end of the roadster market
Price Guide
A £3500   **B** £1800   **C** £700
Current Maker: None

Haydn Davis pioneered the art of the plans-built car in Britain with his Arrow, a traditional 1930s style two-seater. Based as ever on a modified version of the Triumph Herald/Vitesse/Spitfire chassis, though a purpose built chassis (which could also be made at home!) and an MGB option became available. The idea was that you bought a set of paper patterns and plans for peanuts and made the aluminium-skinned plywood body tub yourself. The Arrow had cycle wings, while the later Beretta had flowing GRP wings, which you naturally had to buy from the factory. Some people made exquisite examples.

Burlington Berretta

Following the success of the Arrow, Haydn Davies boosted the package to create the Berretta. It was essentially an Arrow with elegant flowing glassfibre wings and running boards (which cost just £190 plus VAT). The car was designed to be very cheap to finish (£1500 all-in was quoted). You could base it on a Herald chassis, or buy Burlington's own steel chassis and steel body frame. The body is aluminium-skinned plywood with GRP scuttle, rad cowl, dummy tank and wings, aluminium bonnet, wood/ally front valance. Proved to be very popular because of its low cost.

Prod Years: 1985-date
Prod Numbers: Several hundred plans sets
For: Elegant '30s wing line, simple construction, mostly Triumph parts, good value
Against: Doorless, rather basic, standard of build varies greatly, chassis needs careful inspection
Verdict: Handsome budget roadster
Price Guide
A £3500   **B** £1800   **C** £800
Current Maker: None

Burlington Chieftain

An unashamed Willys Jeep replica from the fertile pen of Haydn Davis. Once again, the aluminium-and-plywood body was designed to be made by individual builders working to a set of plans which Burlington sold for ten quid. Similarly, the basis was the backbone chassis/floorpan of the Triumph Herald (LWB) or Spitfire (SWB). GRP scuttle, alloy/plywood body, metal bonnet. But people's imaginations were not fired by the idea of a Spitfire-chassised jeep and sales of plans sets were much lower than those for the Arrow and Berretta. As such, complete cars are rather rare. Something of a precursor to the later and much more popular Husky.

Prod Years: 1983-92
Prod Numbers: Many plans sets
For: Jeep looks, simple Triumph mechanicals
Against: Extremely basic, variable quality of owners' builds, rust in floorpan, rotting woodwork
Verdict: Could be fun but best to avoid cheaply-made ones
Price Guide
A £1600   **B** £800   **C** £300
Current Maker: None

Butterfield Musketeer

This car has the rare distinction of being probably the first ever Mini based kit car. Produced by Butterfield Engineering of Nazeing, Essex, it was offered in two forms: 850 and 1000, both with new Mini engines and components, though mounted in a strong multi-tubular chassis. Swish spec included rev counter, two-speed wipers, flip-forward front end and optional Koni adjustables. Expensive at prices from £848 (nearly twice the price of a Mini), so it's not surprising that it was left to later kits to cash in on the Mini's inherent strengths. Extreme rarity might give it some cachet in Mini circles.

Prod Years: 1961-63
Prod Numbers: Very few
For: Quirk quotient, Mini basis, well conceived and made, quite luxurious for a '60s sports car
Against: Horrid proportions and ugly lines, probably none exists any more
Verdict: Little more than a historical footnote
Price Guide
Too rare to say
Current Maker: None

Calvy Mitchel

Since Calvy started life as NG agents, it's not surprising that its first product should look like the NG TC. However, an eyebrow was raised when it was found that Calvy had duplicated just about everything from the NG, from chassis to body panels, and court action forced a MkII redesign. Hence the Calvy was given a ladder chassis in place of the NG-type cruciform, plus there was a squarer front end and doors. The former two points were demerits, the latter a positive benefit. Like the NG, the mechanical basis was MGB, though Rover V8 power became an option. In its day, it was a moderately popular kit car.

Prod Years: 1983-92
Prod Numbers: Approx 50
For: Quality of glassfibre mouldings high, doors are welcome when compared to an NG
Against: Chassis not really properly sorted (especially for the V8)
Verdict: An NG is a better bet
Price Guide
A £5500   **B** £3200   **C** £1500
Current Maker: None

Clan Crusader

☆☆☆☆☆

Prod Years: 1971-74
Prod Numbers: 325
For: Distinctive style, impeccable steering, roadholding and braking
Against: Harsh ride, cramped inside, slab-sided appearance
Verdict: If any kit car is collectable, the Clan is surely one of the main candidates
Price Guide
A £3500   **B** £2200   **C** £1200
Current Maker: None

Lotus refugee Paul Haussauer built his small GT car with help from some Lotus friends near Norwich, notably stylist John Frayling. Glassfibre monocoque body formed out of upper and lower sections, plus 51bhp Hillman Imp Sport engine and suspension carried on rear subframe, plus Imp front end and Imp-based interior. Large factory in County Durham built type-approved cars at an expensive £1399, though cheaper kits were offered. Just 11.4cwt, so 100mph performance. Spasmodic Chrysler supplies and falling demand killed it. The project was sold to a Cypriot business, using Simca 1000 engines.

Clan

☆☆☆☆☆

Prod Years: 1983-87
Prod Numbers: Approx 100
For: Familiar and semi-classic package, prettier than original Clan, a lot of fun to drive, well made
Against: Imp basis is from a different age, tight fit inside
Verdict: Worthwhile Clan reunion
Price Guide
A £3500   **B** £2000   **C** £1000
Current Maker: None

Ex-aviation and Northern Ireland Development Agency man Peter McCandless set up the revived Clan Cars in Newtownards, Co Down, in 1982 and proceeded to make a modified version of the 1971 Clan Crusader, much to the chagrin of the original makers. Basic body/chassis kits were sold at £1195 plus VAT from 1983 with the ad line: "It's back! And here to stay". The shape looked very familiar, but the interior and front end were new, sporting a deep spoiler and flush pop-up headlamps, the rear 'boot' was flat and the tyres wider. Imp-based, as ever.

Clan Clover

☆☆☆☆☆

Prod Years: 1986-87
Prod Numbers: Approx 35
For: Sweet Alfasud power, handling balance, high standards of engineering and manufacture
Against: Monocoque is difficult to repair, some cars sold 'new' used shagged-out old parts, so don't pay over the odds
Verdict: Clan never did roll in the clover
Price Guide
A £5000   **B** £3000   **C** £1600
Current Maker: None

After making a revised version of the original Imp-engined Clan, the Newtownards, Northern Ireland manufacturer launched the Clan Clover in 1986. This was an attempt to move up-market, as kits were considerably more expensive than the regular Clan, and the company also sold them fully-built. Comprehensively redesigned, with smoother, wider, more aerodynamic bodywork, fatter arches, side skirts and another interior reworking. Most significant change was a switch from rear-mounted Imp power to a mid-mounted Alfa Romeo Alfasud engine and transmission, which sharpened its handling and performance.

Concept Centaur

☆☆☆

Prod Years: 1974-77
Prod Numbers: 26
For: Wild appearance, high quality construction, great handling, ability to get under car park barriers
Against: Ridiculous driving position, dire visibility, not for claustrophobes, other drivers don't know you're there, Imp power falls short of looks
Verdict: Makes *Thunderbirds* look like *Watch With Mother*
Price Guide
A £1400   **B** £1000   **C** £600
Current Maker: None

In 1969, Dennis Adams designed the Probe 15, the world's lowest ever car at just 29in high. Intended production never began, but the Centaur was the next best thing. In 1970, a portly chap called Peter Timpson acquired a second Probe 15 bodyshell, widened it and modified it considerably, notably creating a pair of perspex windows which doubled up as doors. Height went up (to 37in), but so did practicality. Imp basis remained, and body was a tough GRP-and-plywood monocoque with box section and steel tube reinforcement. A 2+2 Centaur Mk2 was developed but the project passed to Pulsar (qv). Condor roadster was stillborn.

Contemporary 427

Home-grown Cobra replicas have always had a stranglehold on the British market, but there were attempts at imports. The Contemporary 427 from the USA was one of the best (and also one of the first and most popular). Fastidiously duplicated in detail, including the cramped cockpit and stainless steel (not chrome) brightwork, although bodywork was glassfibre, not aluminium. Kits were expensive but comprehensive and used many custom-made parts, though a Jaguar diff and front suspension uprights had to be sourced by the builder. Imported in the early 1980s and more successfully from 1990 by ASS. Optional 289/289 FIA/Daytona Coupe versions.

Prod Years: 1979-date (in USA)
Prod Numbers: Very few imported
For: Replication is highly authentic, very good quality, engineering integrity impeccable
Against: American performance parts can be awkward to find, and expensive, inherits AC's cramped cockpit
Verdict: Definitely worth a look if you see one
Price Guide
A £20,000   **B** £13,000   **C** £9000
Current Importer: American Speed Specialties, Beckenham

Copycats C-Type

Copycats was born in 1982, changing its name to Proteus towards the end of the decade. With the C-Type, it established itself as probably the UK's leading classic Jaguar replicator. There were two types: a very expensive aluminium-bodied replica for Jaguar Mk2 parts (and therefore a live rear axle), or a glassfibre body for Jaguar XJ6 parts, which was easier to finish, some two inches wider and boasted IRS. Both versions could be bought fully-built as well as in kit form, though the kits were always at the top end of the field. Prices for the ally car are roughly double those for the GRP car quoted here.

Prod Years: 1982-date
Prod Numbers: Approx 200
For: Exacting authenticity inside and out, superlative standards of chassis engineering and manufacture, glorious to drive
Against: Pretty impractical, expensive
Verdict: One of the best of all classic replicas, Jaguar or otherwise
Price Guide
A £25,000   **B** £17,500   **C** £10,000
Current Maker: Proteus Cars, Little Lever, Bolton

Corry Cultra

After the long-established Welsh sports car maker Davrian went bust, a Northern Irish businessman called Will Corry bought up the remains and set up Corry Cars in Ballynahinch, County Down. The Davrian had already become quite up-market, and the Corry travelled further up. The bodywork was totally restyled by Tony Stevens (who was earlier responsible for the lovely Cipher), and decidedly extraordinary it was, too. Fulfilling its main role as a competition car, the mid-engined sports coupe notched up a few successes in minor rallies but sales of road cars were pitifully few. The Davrian was later revived by Darrian.

Prod Years: 1983-85
Prod Numbers: Few
For: Dynamically proven by Davrian, some rarity value
Against: Looks like a breadvan from the Plant Whacko, body spares could be difficult
Verdict: Weird as they come - would make an interesting mystery car at the pub or an off-beat rally car
Price Guide
A £4000   **B** £3000   **C** £2000
Current Maker: None

Covin

In 1984, Essex-based Covin Performance Mouldings were bold enough to launch a VW Beetle based replica of the then current Porsche 911. Trouble was it was too close for Stuttgart, and they demanded a redesign. The Turbo Coupe was the only model available initially, but a Cabriolet version was soon added (see opposite). Choice of Beetle floorpan or purpose-made chassis, and of VW engines or water-cooled units (Ford Escort XR3 was popular). Also a Rinspeed-style droop-snoot option. In 1992, the production rights went to DJ Sportscars for three years, then to Grannd Performance Cars of Luton.

Prod Years: 1984-95
Prod Numbers: Several hnudred
For: Porsche prestige for budget price, quite well made, can be made to go pretty well, simple mechanicals
Against: Genuine Porkers aren't that much more expensive, early ones had handling problems
Verdict: Not totally convincing
Price Guide
A £7500   **B** £5000   **C** £2200
Current Maker: None

Covin Cabriolet

Prod Years: 1985-96
Prod Numbers: Approx 100
For: You could believe it is a Porker, open top is a plus, find one with a Porsche engine and it even sounds right and goes ok
Against: It will never be a Porsche, Cabriolet is less convincing than Coupe, hood not up to much
Verdict: Passable counterfeit
Price Guide
A £7500   **B** £5000   **C** £2500
Current Maker: None

A drop-top version of the Covin Porsche replica was almost inevitable. The 2+2 seating arrangement was retained, but the roof was lost, to be replaced by a folding top (which was sadly nowhere near the quality and effectiveness of the Porsche item). Same shortened VW floorpan or optional Covin chassis for VW Variant parts (or Ford CVH engines). Same choice of 'traditional' body styling or 'custom' mix-and-match modifications like droop-snoot, wide sills, deep spoilers, etc. In DJ's hands, some nine further Covins were built from 1992 (coupé and cabriolet), but after that it was all downhill for the replica exotic.

CS+2

.Prod Years: 1977-86
Prod Numbers: Approx 50
For: Whackily original looks, great fun, sharp handling, simple Mini bits, cheap to buy and run
Against: Rather crude, not very durable, no doors
Verdict: Much more interesting than a Beetle-based buggy
Price Guide
A £1200   **B** £750   **C** £400
Current Maker: None

Barrie Stimson's original mind created the Minibug (qv) as long ago as 1970 and this crazy-looking projectile was steadily updated to become the CS+II in 1975. He made only two of these before selling the project to Mini Motors of Rochdale in 1977. They renamed the car CS2 in 1979, selling over 40 cars before the project changed hands once more in 1982 (renamed again, as CS+2!). An electric version was being offered alongside the Mini-based one by 1984, when kits cost just £600 + VAT. Despite bargain prices, the CS+2 simply faded away amongst the more sophisticated kit cars of the late '80s.

Cygnet Monaco

Prod Years: 1982-85
Prod Numbers: Approx 10
For: We're struggling
Against: Dismal quality, sad looks, total absence of engineering, daft packaging - do you want us to go on?
Verdict: Why, why, why???
Price Guide
A £900   **B** £500   **C** £100
Current Maker: None

Desperation for a Cortina based four-seater kit was surely the only reason why anyone bought a Cygnet Monaco - and buy them they did. A classic of non-styling, the profile of the Monaco actually sloped upwards towards the front and it also boasted a concave roof. Other curious features were all-flat glass, chiselled-out headlamp apertures and an impressively complete disregard for the word 'quality'. The chap who made them in Newport Pagnell was, incredibly, ex-Aston Martin. A convertible Cygnetina version was planned, but we're not sure if any were made. Of interest only to the most perverse collector of plastic contraptions.

Cygnet Roadster

Prod Years: 1983
Prod Numbers: Probably 1
For: It's unique (phew!)
Against: A litany of objections along the lines of aesthetics, conception, execution, function - that covers just about everything
Verdict: This ugly duckling never turned into a swan
Price Guide
Surely no-one would ask money for it
Current Maker: None

Not satisfied with just one monstrosity, the company called Cygnet Cars proudly displayed a sister model to the abominable Cygnet right at the beginning of its life. At the National Kit Car Show at Stoneleigh in Warwickshire in spring 1983, it showed a traditional style vehicle with flowing (we use the term vaguely) wings, very squared-up bodywork, a removable hardtop and separate rear luggage box. Since nothing more was ever heard of the project (and the company did publicize the Monaco extensively), we presume the Cortina based Roadster remained a one-off. The kit car industry breathed a sigh of relief.

Davrian Imp Mk I/II

Built in 1967 by Adrian Evans, the first proper Davrian was a one-off open sports car with a plywood/glassfibre monocoque body/chassis unit, rear mounted Hillman Imp power and removable hardtop. The Davrian Developments company was born in a Clapham, South London, workshop in 1968, offering same car but with Miura-style flip-up headlights and Mk2 designation. Production version used all-GRP monocoque, Spitfire windscreen and Imp engine and suspension, the engine being mounted directly on to the GRP rear bulkhead. Fixed headlamps optional. Basic body/chassis kit price started at £200, and much D.I.Y. skill was needed.

Prod Years: 1967-70
Prod Numbers: 1/approx 20
For: Excellent handling, light weight, pretty shape, very strong chassis, novelty of open top on first cars
Against: Fairly crude as a road car, accident damage can compromise structure, poor quality mouldings
Verdict: Rare early Davrian which could be worth a close look
Price Guide
A £3000   **B** £2500   **C** £1000
Current Maker: None

Davrian Imp MkIII/IV

While the rear engined (Imp) Davrian progressed to Mk 3 specification, the new Demon was launched at the January 1969 Racing Car Show with fixed head fastback bodywork and mid-mounted Imp power. It seems unlikely the Demon ever got into production; the rear engined model was preferred for simplicity in both manufacture and assembly. Mk4 version came out early in 1970 with fixed head notchback body using almost vertical rear window, front-hinged bonnet and separate engine cover. The proven GRP monocoque was retained, with Imp suspension and steering. Pop-up headlights now standard for road cars.

Prod Years: 1969/1970-71
Prod Numbers: Approx 50/approx 30
For: Proven strength of body/chassis, lively performance, excellent roadholding and handling
Against: Early kit car that's very basic by any standards
Verdict: Interesting early Davrians but best left to fanatics!
Price Guide
A £3000   **B** £2500   **C** £1000
Current Maker: None

Davrian MkV-VII

The MkV Davrian appeared at the January 1971 Racing Car Show, retaining usual styling but notable for rear steel subframe for engine mounting and completely removable rear body moulding for easier engine access. All-GRP monocoque and Imp power and running gear unchanged, but now there was a one-piece, flip-forward front bodywork moulding incorporating the bonnet and new shape pop-up headlight panels. MkVI model only different in detail while MkVII's engine mounting subframe had engine suspended below it. Mini and VW Beetle engined options were offered from early 1973.

Prod Years: 1971-79
Prod Numbers: Approx 400
For: Rally-proven structure, legendary handling, attractive to look at, strong yet very light, easy to live with
Against: Crude in many areas, many have been thrashed
Verdict: Excellent sports car for its day, though those times are fading
Price Guide
A £4700   **B** £2700   **C** £1000
Current Maker: None

Davrian MkVIII/Dragon

The growingly reputable Davrian operation moved factory from London to Wales in 1976, consolidating production of the definitive MkVII. A much revised MkVIII model arrived in 1980, boasting improved styling with reshaped front and rear ends, fixed cowled headlamps, better cockpit room, duraluminium undertray, Davrian-designed four-wheel discs and, most importantly, a mid-mounted engine (usually Ford Fiesta). Kits cost £2800 plus tax but an ambitious plan to sell complete cars as the Dragon, with Welsh Development Agency money, eventually dragged the company down. A sad end for a famous car.

Prod Years: 1980-83
Prod Numbers: Approx 50
For: Highly suitable for dual-purpose competition work, still supported by Team Duffee Engineering
Against: Hard use takes its toll, not the most comfortable sports car you can buy
Verdict: Ultimate expression of the original Davrian
Price Guide
A £5000   **B** £2800   **C** £1100
Current Maker: None

Dax 427/Tojeiro

☆☆☆☆☆☆

Prod Years: 1979-date
Prod Numbers: Approx 1700
For: Solid reputation built up over many years, tough chassis, excellent build quality, accuracy of repro parts, high resale value
Against: Expensive compared to other 427 replicas
Verdict: The original - and still the best bet second-hand
Price Guide
A £22,500   **B** £16,000   **C** £8000
Current Maker: DJ Sportscars, Harlow, Essex

DJ Sportscars was the first British company to tackle a replica of the 427 Cobra, making its first two-piece GRP shell in 1979. The enthusiastic staff did most of the work making a viable 427 replica, developing many repro parts, chassis for Ford or Jaguar axles and a huge variety of engines, from Ford V6 up to American V8s. The AC Ace chassis designer, John Tojeiro, became a director of DJ in 1985 and the car was renamed in his honour. Eventual options included ladder or square tube or racing 'Supertube' space frame chassis, Jag V12 power and 400bhp+ engines. Wide variety of interpretations, from faithful to high-tech.

Deep Sanderson

☆☆☆☆☆

Prod Years: 1963-64
Prod Numbers: 14
For: Well-developed chassis, Le Mans heritage, good looks, race-bred kudos
Against: Cramped, extremely rare and hard to find
Verdict: Classic racer for the road – one of the desirable early kit cars
Price Guide
A £5000   **B** £3500   **C** £1800
Current Maker: None

Famous Morgan tuner and racer Chris Lawrence founded Deep Sanderson in 1960, tackling the manufacture of Formula Junior cars. The prototype racing 301 was built in 1961, a particularly ugly open-topped device (nicknamed 'perfume delivery wagon'), thankfully restyled into a good looking coupe for its 1963 launch as a road car. Backbone chassis, steel tube frame, aluminium floor, GRP bodywork – all for £750 in kit form. Engines were mid-mounted Mini-Cooper units, suspension was bespoke. The car is only 36in high but has the distinction of being a Le Mans runner in '63 and '64. Virtually extinct now, sadly.

Delkit Camino

☆☆☆

Prod Years: 1984-85
Prod Numbers: Approx 6
For: Engineering was quite sound, strong chassis, thick bodyshell, proper moulded interior, vast boot
Against: Unfortunately looks rather like a pregnant Beetle
Verdict: Potentially good but actually slightly embarrassing
Price Guide
A £1200   **B** £700   **C** £300
Current Maker: None

A Telford-based ex-army officer called Derek Allen was behind the Camino, which was created by boat builder John Rock. It had the potential to be a good car: it was an early example of a Cortina MkIII/IV based coupe (virtually all the parts came from this donor), the mould quality was good, the interior looked professional, the ladder chassis was very strong and incorporated a sheet steel backbone. The problem was the styling, or lack of it: it was over-heavy, bulbous and unsubtle, making it hard to believe the company's puff that the lines were "flawless" and that this was "the ultimate kit car design".

DG Phoenix

☆☆☆

Prod Years: 1982-date
Prod Numbers: Approx 400
For: It's guaranteed to get attention, can be made to go indecently fast, it's very simple and cheap to run, you don't have to wear a helmet
Against: The rain goes straight down your front
Verdict: Some of the pleasures of biking were retained, but it was really a fair-weather friend only
Price Guide
A £2500   **B** £1500   **C** £500
Current Maker: DG Motor Services

Custom trikes are more the province of American bikers than British ones, since the thought of travelling on a rainy day down the M62 in one hardly inspires visions of *Easy Rider*. But one UK company has consistently satisfied domestic demands. Stick a VW Beetle engine in a basic box section chassis, add extended motorbike front forks and a basic two-seater GRP body and, hey presto, you have a trike that can be driven on a 'bike licence. DG also made a US-style off-road rail from its premises in Wellingborough, Northants (only half a dozen were sold).

Dial Buccaneer

★★☆☆☆

There were a number of racing orientated mid-engined kit cars around the beginning of the 1970s, of which the Dial Buccaneer was perhaps the most successful. That's not saying much, as it was virtually unbuildable. It used a wide variety of parts in a space frame chassis: Triumph based independent suspension all round, VW gearbox, Ford in-line engines. The glassfibre bodywork looked iffy and mould quality wasn't up to much, while the gullwing doors were a pain to fit. Moreover, there are no recorded instances of any competition success, so quite why you'd want to own a Buccaneer is a bit of a mystery.

Prod Years: 1970-71
Prod Numbers: Very few
For: Rarity value, light weight, good handling
Against: Shoddy quality, pig ugly styling, impossible to find spare parts
Verdict: No more than an oddity - do any still exist, we wonder?
Price Guide
Difficult to say, but cheap
Current Maker: None

Diva GT

★★★★★

Don Sim asked Heron Plastics of Greenwich to modify a Heron Europa bodyshell to show off his Tunex Ford 998cc engine, primarily as a racing car. Other drivers showed an interest, so Divas went into production from 1962. The specification included a space frame chassis, and Tunex or Ford Classic engines and most examples were built for racing. The 'D' Type of 1965 had an extended nose, wider wheels and bigger brakes, while the 10F variant of 1966 was a pure road car, featuring thicker glassfibre and an insulated engine. There was also a Valkyr model, but only six were made in 1965-66 (see below).

Prod Years: 1962-67
Prod Numbers: Approx 80
Fors: Race-proven chassis (class win at Nurburgring 1968), enthusiastic current ownership, eminently eligible for historic racing
Against: Crude as a road car
Verdict: Hairy racing-orientated sports cars
Price Guide
Probably £3000-£12000
Current Maker: None

Diva Valkyr

★★★★★

Diva's mid-engined race car could also be driven on the road. Its first appearance was at the 1965 Racing Car Show where it was displayed as the Demon, a pure road car powered by a Hillman Imp engine in a space frame chassis. This was soon converted to Lotus Cortina 1500 power and became the Valkyr production model. This retained the space frame construction but had improved suspension and different wings and windscreen. Cosworth engines (up to 300bhp!) were optional. Of the six cars built, two were exported, leaving Diva's last model as a total rarity.

Prod Years: 1965-68
Prod Numbers: 6
For: Dramatic shape, impressive competitiion record and eligibility for historic racing, collector status
Against: Extreme rarity, something of a crudity as a road machine
Verdict: Delectable piece of 1960s race machinery
Price Guide
Impossible to quote, but expensive
Current Maker: None

Dragonfly

★★★★☆

Like the Arkley SS, the Dragonfly was a way to turn your MG Midget into something that looked completely different. The central body was left untouched, but the rear end was removed and replaced with a rounded GRP moudling. The front part of the chassis was lengthened by over 10in, which meant that the front suspension had to be softened and moved forward and the steering column extended. A new tapering bonnet, flowing wings with vestigial running boards and a new radiator shell were fitted (all in glassfibre). Marketing by the Hampshire makers was rather lazy, making the Dragonfly an undeserved rarity.

Prod Years: 1981-86
Prod Numbers: Approx 15
For: Well balanced appearance, quality of GRP panels, decent hood and interior courtesy of MG
Against: Less luggage space than the Midget, check that the chassis extension is sound, rust likely in centre section
Verdict: Treat it as a mini Panther Lima, great value
Price Guide
A £4000   B £2500   C £1500
Current Maker: None

Dri-Sleeve Moonraker

☆☆☆☆☆

Prod Years: 1971-72
Prod Numbers: 6
For: Immaculate presentation and beautiful detailing, high quality of manufacture, alloy body, practical mechanicals, good handling
Against: Rough ride, long since out of production
Verdict: So much better than the VW Beetle based Bugatti replicas that followed it
Price Guide
A £9000   **B** £6000   **C** £2500
Current Maker: None

Ryder Slone, Boris Willison and Peter Jackson set up shop in the old Opus premises at Warminster in 1970 and built their Bugatti Type 35 replica. Called Dri-Sleeve because a sleeve was supplied to protect the driver's right arm from the elements. Ladder chassis used a Ford rear axle, modified VW Beetle front end and Ford Cortina 1600GT engine (optionally supercharged to deliver 113bhp). Main body and bonnet in aluminium, detachable rear end, side panels and cycle wings in GRP. Only the fat alloys and Cortina instruments gave it away. At £1954, it was far too expensive to score much sales success.

Dutton P1

☆☆☆

Prod Years: 1970-71
Prod Numbers: 9
For: Light weight so good performance, Sprite parts easy to find, simple construction, aluminium body is rust-free
Against: Extremely stark and crude, rough and ready construction
Verdict: A historic machine in a way, now extremely rare
Price Guide
Difficult to quote
Current Maker: None

Tim Dutton-Woolley began an illustrious kit car making career after building a Lotus based coupe called the Mantis in 1969. He created a cheap kit in the Lotus 7 vein in 1970, which he called the Dutton P1, and formed Dutton Cars in Fontwell, Sussex. Flat aluminium body panels bolted on to a space frame chassis, while glassfibre Lotus 7 wings were used with a specially-made GRP nose, so the styling looked quite close to the Lotus. The mechanical basis was Austin-Healey Sprite Mk1/2. Kits were cheap at around £200 each but the Sprite was already becoming collectable by this stage, so only nine P1s were made.

Dutton B-Type

☆☆☆

Prod Years: 1971-74
Prod Numbers: Approx 250
For: Only 9½cwt, reasonable handling, good looks à la Lotus 7, can be made to perform
Against: Spine-jarring ride, spartan interior, questionable quality
Verdict: This early Dutton has some charms - but don't expect much sophistication
Price Guide
A £2000   **B** £1200   **C** £600
Current Maker: None

A new basis for what looked very much like the P1: the B-Type used Triumph Herald running gear and a Triumph Herald/Spitfire engine (though customers also fitted BMC, Ford and Alfa Romeo power trains). Bodywork now mostly in glassfibre (only the side panels remained aluminium), and a one-piece bonnet/nose was used. ID features are sidelights in recesses on the front wings and indicators on each side of the nose-cone. Kits with full hood were just £295. Hardtop from '72, Ford Anglia van rear axle option from '73. Gradually edged out by the much improved B-Plus.

Dutton B-Plus/B-Plus S2

☆☆☆

Prod Years: 1973-78/1986-89
Prod Numbers: Approx 250
For: A little more refined than the B-Type, still a lot of fun, a V6 version will do 0-60 in 6.4 secs!
Against: Still massively uncomfortable, crude construction, will no doubt require lots of rebuilding
Verdict: Still more 'minus' than 'plus'
Price Guide
A £2000   **B** £1100   **C** £500
Current Maker: None

Redesigned and more substantial chassis created the B-Plus, which initially sold alongside the B-Type for a small premium. Much larger range of power units, though most popular was undoubtedly the Ford 1600 (V6 engines could also be squeezed in). Ford Cortina live rear axle standard. B-Plus body was slightly larger than the B-Type, though still aluminium-and-GRP. Front wings now had no sidelights and the indicators faced forwards. Enclosed round front arch option 1974; with new sloping rear end this was called Malaga (see next page). B-Plus S2 was launched in 1986 with Phaeton chassis and body mods.

Dutton Malaga

The Malaga name, chosen because Tim Dutton tested the prototype in Spain, first appeared on a curved front wing B-Plus in 1974, but only one such car was made. The production Malaga was a complete body option for the B-Plus: enclosed front wings and a sloping, classically-inspired tail in place of the B-Plus' upswept, bespoilered tail. In fact, the front and rear ends of the B-Plus and Malaga were interchangeable, although what you called such cross-breeds no-one ever said! Body/chassis kits cost the same (at £295 + VAT) and the Ford-derived mechanical basis was identical.

Prod Years: 1975-78
Prod Numbers: Approx 200
For: Looks different from other Duttons like the B-Plus and Phaeton, V6 3-litre ones had a certain reputation for thrills – and spills?
Against: This was crude even by the standards of 1970s kit cars let alone today
Verdict: Might be worth a look as a cheapie Seven
Price Guide
A £2000   **B** £1100   **C** £500
Current Maker: None

Dutton Cantera

Tim Dutton-Woolley departed from his Lotus 7 lookalike style with the extraordinary Cantera, which was built as a test-bed for new ideas, though it actually entered production. Modified B-Plus chassis was clothed in an unusual glassfibre coupe body: cut-off tail and squared-off front end with bizarre lighting arrangement. Two seats, proper doors, lots of cabin space. Lightweight (11cwt), so good performance from wide range of engines (usually Ford). Standard Dutton suspension arrangement of Triumph front/Ford rear ends. Kits were not cheap at £475, so this car was always a highly marginal Dutton model.

Prod Years: 1976-77
Prod Numbers: 11
For: At least it's distinctive, it's got a roof and doors
Against: Ride akin to sledging over pot-holes, it really is one of the most bloody ugly things you've seen
Verdict: Real rarity for the truly determined Dutton collector (if such people really do exist)
Price Guide
A £1100   **B** £700   **C** £400
Current Maker: None

Dutton Sierra

Journalist Peter Filby suggested the Sierra idea to Tim Dutton and stylist Richard Oakes designed this ground-breaking estate in 1979. Usual ladder type chassis, though 'on stilts'. Designed around Ford Escort parts (including windscreen and doors), though any Ford engine could be used. Ford took court action over the name. Tall at 64in, but very capacious and a zillion times more practical than any other kit car around, with its opening tail-gate and four seats. Panel van followed. Popular as farm business transport: at £825, kits were good value. Ended up at Hamilton Automotive. Best selling kit of all time?

Prod Years: 1979-92
Prod Numbers: Approx 3000
For: Very practical, four seats, decent Richard Oakes design, rust-proof GRP body
Against: Smaller than you might imagine, high loading lip, not very well made, crude engineering, many now look very shabby, no parts now available
Verdict: Sierra Nirvana? Made sense as a kit, but wouldn't an Escort estate be better second-hand?
Price Guide
A £2300   **B** £1200   **C** £500
Current Maker: None

Dutton Sierra Pick-Up/Chassis Cab

Tim Dutton had his sights set on new territories with the commercial variants of the Sierra: he first advertised them in *Farmer's Weekly*, and kit car builders took a while to cotton on. The Pick-Up was identical to the estate version of the Sierra except for its rear bulkhead and pick-up rear end, and was considerably cheaper. The very basic chassis/cab version eschewed the pick-up bed, leaving the chassis bare for whatever rear bodywork you wanted - box van, flat bed, artic, ice cream cab... Donor vehicle for engine, rear axle and all suspension remained the Ford Escort.

Prod Years: 1981-89
Prod Numbers: Included in Sierra
For: Simplicity, more honest as a pick-up than as a trendy estate, Escort parts are cheap and plentiful
Against: Not really durable enough (most old Sierras have deteriorated badly), quite small, lots of body roll
Verdict: Might make a cheap, rust-free and versatile workhorse
Price Guide
A £1500   **B** £800   **C** £300
Current Maker: None

Dutton Sierra Drophead

Prod Years: 1984-92
Prod Numbers: Included in Sierra
For: A rare example of a true four-seater convertible, looks as funky as a Suzuki jeep, cheap to run
Against: The idea was better than the reality - crude, draughty, leaky, uncomfortable, unrefined
Verdict: Probably better than a beach buggy – just about!
Price Guide
A £2500   **B** £1300   **C** £600
Current Maker: None

While the Escort based Sierra estate and van were doing very well, the Drophead slotted in as a logical and ultimately popular model. The sills were raised (the doors became floppy curtains) and the upper bodywork was removed; a special roll-bar and indented rear end were added. There was less to it, so body/chassis prices were cheaper (£749 plus tax compared with £999 for the estate). A full hood was offered as an option, and later a proper hardtop with solid doors. Became the most popular of all Sierra options and therefore one of the UK's best-selling kits ever.

Dutton Phaeton S1/S2

Prod Years: 1978-82
Prod Numbers: Approx 1500
For: Funky looks, simple mechanically, can be made to go fast and corner well, high fun-per-quid ratio
Against: Pretty crude in all respects, engineering quality was on holiday most of the way, poor glassfibre body mouldings
Verdict: Cheap and can be made to be cheerful
Price Guide
A £3000   **B** £1600   **C** £600
Current Maker: None

Rationalised Dutton model designed to accept mostly Ford Escort parts, though still using Triumph front suspension and wide range of engine possibilities (eg Fiat, Vauxhall, Alfa, Triumph etc). Twin-rail chassis modified to yield extra 3in of cockpit space. Had B-Plus style front with optional (and almost inevitable) spoiler. Cheap kit prices meant astronomic sales (200 in first six months!). Model was lightly improved with the S2 version. The Phaeton was Europe's best selling kit car at this time but was quickly overtaken during the 1980s by rising standards in the industry.

Dutton Phaeton S3/S4

Prod Years: 1982-89
Prod Numbers: Approx 1500
For: Ford suspension gives better ride and handling than S2/S3, wide variety of engines, can be a lot of fun for not much money
Against: Lack of street cred, highly variable quality, not the most sophisticated package around
Verdict: High on fun-per-pound, low on ultimate worth
Price Guide
A £3000   **B** £1600   **C** £600
Current Maker: Eagle Cars

The Series 3 Phaeton arrived at the 1982 Motorfair in London, the chief change being an all-new space frame chassis which switched from Triumph-based front suspension to all-round Escort Mk1 basis. As ever, kits were ultra-cheap (£665) - and ultra-basic. An unusual estate-type hardtop was offered from 1983. The 1989 S4 gained a slightly revised front end and improved rear suspension layout which allowed an extra 6in of legroom. S4 only lasted one season, as Tim Dutton pulled the plug on his empire. Eagle Cars of Arundel, Sussex, revived it in the '90s as the P21/P25.

Dutton Rico

Prod Years: 1984-89
Prod Numbers: 25
For: Very cheap, half-decent road manners, semi practical
Against: Very unrefined, very ugly, very poorly made, very unpleasant
Verdict: You can smell the Rico half-bakedness a mile off
Price Guide
A £800   **B** £500   **C** £250
Current Maker: None

The scale model of Dutton's bold new coupe looked quite promising, but the reality was the opposite. Dumpy styling was compromised by using Escort front glass and certainly did not 'match a production car', as Dutton stated, while the interior was pretty cramped for four. Originally used De Lorean quad headlamps but Series 2 restyle of 1985 had Escort Mk3 lights. Any Ford engine up to a V6 could be used, though the mechanical basis was Escort Mk1/2. Disappointing sales relegated it to the 'special order only' list, as the Shuttle (Rico/Sierra cross-over) version was launched in 1986 (see Volume 4).

Dutton Melos

In Dutton's best year yet (1981), it launched the Melos at Motorfair. This was another Richard Oakes design, though Dutton himself had completed it. It was a 2+2 open sports car whose curvaceous wings and sprouting headlamps suggested a traditional/funster cross-over style. Basis was the Ford Escort Mk1 and indeed the chassis was all but identical to the Phaeton's. At a launch price of £725, kits were considerably more expensive than the Phaeton, which partly explains why it was never quite as popular, even after an S2 redesign (colour-matched bumpers and redesigned bonnet). Later offered by Mantis Cars, then Scorhill Motors.

Prod Years: 1981-95
Prod Numbers: Approx 1500
For: Four seats (but only just), cheap open sports thrills, still very light weight, good performance
Against: Funny-looking, rear seats ludicrously cramped, quality generally not up to much
Verdict: Melos on Wheels - that means basically not very exciting
Price Guide
A £2700   **B** £1500   **C** £600
Current Maker: None

Eagle SS

The American Cimbria SS - itself a derivative of the British Nova - was modified in the UK to become the Eagle SS, launched by Alan Breeze (a cousin of Tim Dutton). Gullwing doors and Porsche 928-style pop-up headlamps were attention-grabbers, but the standard VW floorpan was not. So Eagle designed a new tubular steel ladder chassis for Ford Cortina MkIII/IV components in 1983 (the front subframe and rear axle bolted straight in). Unfortunately, the front-mounted engine meant a large bonnet bulge was necessary, especially with the V6 engine fitted. Massive popularity waned as the years went by.

Prod Years: 1981-date
Prod Numbers: Approx 600
For: Dramatic styling, cheap prices
Against: Avoid VW based cars, quality usually iffy, gullwing doors were poorly sealed on earlier cars because the roof sagged
Verdict: Primitive cool
Price Guide
A £4000   **B** £2500   **C** £800
Current Maker: Eagle Cars, Arundel, Sussex

Eagle +2

By the time the limitations of the gullwing-doored SS began to show through, Eagle had already developed a new version. The +2 was a four-seater which also had a convertible roof, flat rear deck with opening boot lid, revised windscreen arrangement and a roll-over bar. Naturally the gullwing doors had to go, being replaced by conventional doors. However, there were no winding windows (typical of the half-baked nature of the car). Another difference was covered headlamps instead of pop-ups. There was no VW based version, only one using Ford Cortina parts, as per the SS. Overall, not as attractive as the SS.

Prod Years: 1983-90
Prod Numbers: Approx 50
For: *Al fresco* motoring, no VW option, four seats (just)
Against: Incoherent style, unfinished design, poor quality all round
Verdict: Plus: two rear seats. Minus: two points in every other area
Price Guide
A £2500   **B** £1600   **C** £600
Current Maker: None

Eagle RV/4x4/DB50

Eagle took over the Rhino (qv) in 1983, broadening its base of Beetle-based kits. It was renamed RV and, within months, received its own purpose-built ladder chassis for Cortina mechanicals. The RV had a standard roll cage, plus options of soft or hard tops, bull bars, soft or hard doors, etc. In 1985, Eagle's AWDC advocate, Rob Budd, developed a 4x4 version based on the mechanicals of the Range Rover (the first kit ever to use this donor), which could be had with Eagle's own chassis or with the Range Rover's. A Daihatsu Fourtrak based version called the DB50 arrived in 1992, and a Sierra option in late 1994.

Prod Years: 1983-date
Prod Numbers: Approx 1000
For: Rugged styling, good ground clearance, 4x4 versions excellent off-road, plenty of space inside
Against: Early ones were rather underdeveloped and of dodgy quality, generally unsophisticated
Verdict: Tough no-frills cookie - 4x4 ones are best
Price Guide
A £4500   **B** £2500   **C** £800
Current Maker: Eagle Cars, Arundel, Sussex

Elva Courier MkI

☆☆☆☆☆☆

Prod Years: 1958-59
Prod Numbers: Approx 50
For: Handsome lines, fine handling, can be made to go very quickly, solid image, classic status
Against: Rather rugged and basic, somewhat antique in feel, very rarely offered for sale
Verdict: Has a strong following, and it's not difficult to see why
Price Guide
A £6500   **B** £4500   **C** £3000
Current Maker: None

The first Elva Courier appeared in 1958 as a pretty but basic sports car from a firm which had already scored many notable competition successes on the race track. It used a tubular ladder chassis, Riley 1.5 or MGA engines, Triumph based suspension, rigid rear axle with coil springs, and a well made glassfibre body. MkI Couriers are easily identified by their split windscreens and different dash layout. Most of the production went to America but there were limited sales in Britain in kit form. American Elvas scored some notable racing successes, causing them to be lumped in with E-Types in later years.

Elva Courier MkII

☆☆☆☆☆☆

Years: 1959-61
Prod Numbers: Approx 350
For: MG engine, standards of manufacture, charming style and character, a real sports car in every sense
Against: Hard ride, crude controls, rare and expensive
Verdict: Great British sports car
Price Guide
A £6500   **B** £4500   **C** £3000
Current Maker: None

The much improved MkII Courier arrived in 1959, featuring a new chassis designed to accept the MGA 1622cc engine (100mph top speed and 0-60mph in 10 secs). Also new was a one-piece curved windscreen and improved weather gear. Comprehensive kits were properly offered in the UK from 1960, though most production continued to go abroad. A hardtop was shown at the 1961 Racing Car Show but Elva Engineering sadly went bust that year and so none was made. The pieces were picked up by the Croydon based Trojan company, who developed the MkIII.

Elva Courier MkIII

☆☆☆☆☆☆

Prod Years: 1962-65
Prod Numbers: Approx 100
For: Familiar Elva virtues, purist sports car character, simplified suspension
Against: Same old hard ride, chassis was not well received, having some roadholding problems
Verdict: Still an absolute classic
Price Guide
A £6500   **B** £4500   **C** £3000
Current Maker: None

Trojan Ltd formed Elva Cars (1961) Ltd on taking over Frank Nichols' road car concern and soon developed a new MkIII. The standard Elva tubular ladder chassis was redesigned to accept Triumph Herald front suspension, front discs, MG or Ford power. Kits now cost £716, and there was a new hardtop coupe model (pictured) at £738, distinctive for its quirky reverse-angle rear, *a la* Ford Anglia (though only 10 of these notchback coupes were ever made - in 1962 only). The popular MkIII roadster continued in production alongside the later MkIV, also introduced in 1962 (see below).

Elva Courier MkIV/T-Type

☆☆☆☆☆☆

Prod Years: 1962-67
Prod Numbers: Approx 100
For: Far more practical than earlier Couriers, much better suspension makes for better ride and handling, more balanced styling
Against: Still not as sophisticated as other sports car rivals, they are very rare in the UK
Verdict: The best Courier of all
Price Guide
A £7500   **B** £5000   **C** £3000
Current Maker: None

The restyled Courier MkIV appeared in late 1962 with 2+2 seating and a fastback coupe option. Within a year, the new T-Type MkIV superseded it. This had Tru-Trak independent rear suspension (eventually IFS too), a larger boot and an MGB 1798cc engine (optional Cortina GT 1558cc - up to 140bhp!). Trojan sold out to Ken Sheppard Sports Cars in 1965. This company made only the T-Type 1800 roadster, but only produced 26 of them before petering into nothingness. Sebring Courier is lightweight racing version. So-called Courier 3000 coupé was a later one-off, and the last Elva of all.

Emery GT

Paul Emery's compact and unusual looking GT was the very first special to be based on the Hillman Imp, and appeared in 1963. The very low (40in) glassfibre body (aluminium on the prototype) was bonded on to a neat space frame chassis. Conventional coil/spring damper and wishbone suspension was improved by anti-dive and anti-squat geometry. Mid-mounted Imp or Ford 1050cc engines provided great performance in the 10cwt Emery GT. Some track successes were scored in 1966, but the death of Emery's financier sealed the car's fate. Only two cars remained in the UK.

Prod Years: 1963-64
Prod Numbers: 4
For: Very rigid structure, very light weight, exemplary handling, reasonably spacious for two people
Against: Finding one will be a major problem, rather unrefined
Verdict: Perhaps the ultimate Imp-based specialist GT car
Price Guide
Very hard to fix
Current Maker: None

EPC Hustler

Although it is today a completely forgotten name, Essex Proto Conversions of Chelmsford (and later Dagenham) was once one of the major kit car players, surfing the beach buggy wave. The standard Hustler was very GP-like but the GT version (at £5 extra!) had a curved windscreen and close-set faired-in headlamps. Both were for short-wheelbase VW pans (12in chop). Another feature was spats over the front and rear wheels which made the fashionably fat rubber of the period legal. There was also a side cover panel which helped it become "the greatest looking buggy" (according to the makers).

Prod Years: 1970-72
Prod Numbers: Several hundred
For: GT looked different to other bugs, still a lot of fun, better made
Against: That's not saying much, and it's bound to be little more than shagged out candidate with which to make an interesting pond
Verdict: Find one with purple metalflake paint and a Gary Glitter 8-track cartridge - you know it's cool
Price Guide
A £1200   **B** £600   **C** £300
Current Maker: None

EPC Pinza GS

Most buggies were boring Meyers Manx/GP Buggy rip-offs, but at least they sold well. EPC's Pinza GS was an object lesson for the wisdom of sticking with what you know. As a sports/buggy crossover, the Pinza was adventurous, if nothing else. But the styling was... well, you decide for yourself. The basis was an unshortened Beetle chassis and you got a fitted windscreen, dashboard and heater for your 180 quid (complete cars were marketed at £650, no less). 2 or 4 seats. EPC offered 100 colours for it (most of them shades of metalflake lime green), and there was also an optional hard top with gullwing doors.

Prod Years: 1970-72
Prod Numbers: Very few
For: Actually quite well made, standard Beetle gear, it won't be mistaken for anything else
Against: You might be mistaken for a dipstick though, so many wobbly lines it ought to be breathalysed
Verdict: Where on earth did they get that name?
Price Guide
A £1000   **B** £600   **C** £100
Current Maker: None

Eurocco

The most convoluted story in kitcardom begins in 1978 at Mike Carlton's Embeesea Cars, makers of the famous Charger. Richard Oakes styled the initial notchback Eurocco, but Embeesea never put it on sale (later it became the SN1 - see page 96). Instead Embeesea gave it a fastback roof in 1981, but glass problems led to a 1982 redesign with windows in the previously blank rear three-quarter panels. Based on a VW floorpan (later Alfasud/Lancia engine options). Embeesea gave up making cars in 1984 and the following year Roy Coates of S&R Sports Cars produced new versions called the SR1 and SR2 (see page 97).

Prod Years: 1981-84
Prod Numbers: A handful
For: Interesting shape, simple mechanics, four seats
Against: Eurocco was never very well developed, VW mechanicals a drag
Verdict: One of the industry's also rans and to be avoided
Price Guide
A £2700   **B** £1500   **C** £700
Current Maker: None

EWM Buccaneer

Prod Years: 1984-85/1988-89
Prod Numbers: A few
For: Simple design and mechanicals, should be very cheap
Against: Crudity of design and manufacture, hideous to look at, long since out of production so replacement panels are unavailable
Verdict: Run away
Price Guide
A £1000   B £600   C £400
Current Maker: None

At the height of the huge popularity of the Dutton Phaeton, Edward Waddington decided to launch a competitor in the budget roadster market. The result was frankly a bit of lash-up. The styling was definitely out of the shoe box school of design, but at least the Ford Cortina basis and cheap kit prices were in its favour. Of the two models offered, the Buccaneer was the 'trad' model with a squarish nose. A Birmingham firm called B&S Sports Cars revived the Buccaneer as the Roadster in 1988, but the design was even more out-of-step with current trends by then and the car quickly faded away.

EWM Brigand

Prod Years: 1984-85/1988-89
Prod Numbers: Very few
For: More unusual than a Dutton Phaeton and probably cheaper too
Against: Nasty styling thanks to mishmash of straight lines and curves, no doors, very crude in most areas
Verdict: The sort of car that gives people who laugh about kit cars all the ammunition they need
Price Guide
A £1000   B £600   C £400
Current Maker: None

Rather like the 1970s Dutton range, EWM made two models by interchanging the front and rear ends, which were made of glassfibre, while the metal centre section remained the same. Hence the Cortina donor vehicle was also unchanged. Whereas the Buccaneer was loosely 'traditional' in style, the Brigand was equally loosely 'sporting', with its droop snoot, deep front spoiler, four headlamps and ridiculously large rear spoiler. Birmingham based B&S Sports Cars revived the Brigand as the BS Sprint in 1988 but by then it was an outmoded no-hoper.

Fairthorpe Atomota/Atom Major

Prod Years: 1957-59
Prod Numbers: Approx 30
For: Novelty value (only two are known to exist today)
Against: It's ugly, crude, cramped, noisy; even if that doesn't put you off, you won't be able to find one anyway
Verdict: Unique and ultra-rare piece of British sports car history
Price Guide
Impossible to quote due to rarity
Current Maker: None

Air Vice-Marshall 'Pathfinder' Bennett started making cars with the 1954 Atom, an unbearably crude rear-engined microcar (but this was never sold in kit form). The follow-up Atomota was basically the same car with giant rear fins and a 646cc BSA twin mounted at the opposite (ie front) end. The bodywork was glassfibre, the chassis a backbone, the suspension all-independent and the gearbox an all-sychro four-speeder. If that sounds sophisticated for the 1950s, it was, but in practice the Atomota was anything but. The Atom Major derivative model had a Standard 8/10 engine.

Fairthorpe Electron

Prod Years: 1956-62
Prod Numbers: 20
For: Authentic '50s flavour, not unattractive, so much more interesting than an old Spitfire or Midget
Against: Pretty basic stuff, you'll have a tough job tracking one down
Verdict: Something distinctly superior to the average '50s special
Price Guide
A £5000   B £3000   C £1600
Current Maker: None

A basic twin-rail chassis designed for TR2 suspension, a glassfibre body supplied by Microplas and an on-the-road price price of £995 was the recipe for the Electron. Since a TR2 cost only £787, it was perhaps better to wait for the 1958 complete kit version (at £734). Engine options included Climax, Butterworth 1.5-litre and Standard 10. Later (post-1958) ones had Electron Minor bodywork with a longer nose, and some had bog Standard suspension. Fairthorpe had to persuade buyers that this was not a crude 'special' but a convincing MG/Triumph rival - with little success. There are very few known survivors, and most were exported to the USA.

Fairthorpe Electron Minor

☆☆☆☆

The smoth looking EM (Electron Minor) was a good idea: a compact sports car with its own tublar steel ladder chassis and proprietary parts, predating the Austin-Healey Sprite. Mechanically, the EM used Standard 10 suspension and 38bhp engine from the same source – not powerful, but the EM was a lightweight 9 cwt, and tuning was available. Shorter wheelbase than the Electron, and different nose treatment. Very cheap too – £450 in complete kit form. 45bhp Triumph Herald engines from 1959, which made the EM much faster (90mph+). This is the Fairthorpe which you are most likely to find these days.

Prod Years: 1957-60
Prod Numbers: Approx 300
For: Classic sports car ambience, no pretensions whatsoever, can be made to perform these days
Against: Desperately crude, early EMs are rare
Verdict: A devoted following exists for the little Fairthorpes
Price Guide
A £4000   **B** £2700   **C** £1300
Current Maker: None

Fairthorpe EM2

☆☆☆☆

The end of production of the Standard 10 on which the EM was based heralded a change at Fairthorpe - literally, since the Triumph Herald was the new donor, suspension and all. Thus the EM2's chassis was a little wider, allowing alternative engines to be fitted (eg Ford Anglia, Prefect and Consul). The distinctive double-vent bonnet was new too (taken from the Zeta), and a later option had a single oval intake. Rear suspension was Herald or optional beam axle and coil/overs. Kit prices went up to £498, but already the EM's heyday was over and sales were plummeting.

Prod Years: 1960-63
Prod Numbers: Approx 50
For: Quicker and better handling than the first EM, prettier and less crude inside too, lots of classic pure driving fun
Against: By any standards this is pretty basic transportation
Verdict: Affordable classic sports car
Price Guide
A £4000   **B** £2700   **C** £1300
Current Maker: None

Fairthorpe EM3/EM4/EM5/EM6

☆☆☆

A longer wheelbase, Morris Oxford windscreen and a nose from the Rockette Mk2 distinguished the attractive EM3 of 1963. Still Triumph based, and Herald or the new 1147cc Spitfire engines could be used, as well as the popular and tunable Ford units. EM4 of 1965 had a rejigged chassis and 1296cc Spitfire power. The EM5 of 1970 had a longer tail (therefore making it a 2+2) and Viva windscreen. Final EM6 - also 1970 - used an entire Triumph GT6 chassis in place of Fairthorpe's own, but by now it was ever-decreasing circles: only 2 examples of the EM6 were made.

Prod Years: 1963-65/1965-70/ 1970/1970-73
Prod Numbers: Approx 30/10/5/2
For: Quicker and better handling than the first EM, prettier and less crude inside too, lots of classic pure driving fun
Against: By any standards this is pretty basic transportation
Verdict: Affordable classic sports car
Price Guide
A £4000   **B** £2700   **C** £1300
Current Maker: None

Fairthorpe Electrina

☆☆

As if the Atomota had not been a cautionary experience, Fairthorpe founder Don Bennett proceeded to make another odd saloon, this time based on the EM2. Bulbous all-new rear bodywork - the roof was moulded from a Mk1 Jag - enabled the fitment of a rear bench seat, while the rear wheel arches gained an odd forward-slant. You got full doors (with such luxuries as door handles and sliding windows) which contained an adjustable bar to make the door fit the aperture! Choice of Electron or Zeta noses, and indicators and wipers were extra! Running gear was from the Triumph Herald. Survivors are almost unheard-of.

Prod Years: 1960-63
Prod Numbers: 6
For: It's unusual to say the least, you get four seats and an opening boot and surely the world's only pair of adjustable doors!
Against: All but extinct, horribly ugly, just as crude as other Fairthorpes but without the joy of open-top sports driving
Verdict: A disappointing aberration
Price Guide
Impossible to quote
Current Maker: None

Fairthorpe Zeta

☆☆☆☆

Prod Years: 1959-63
Prod Numbers: 5
For: Infamous performance (certainly one of the fastest cars around in 1959), it's worth having one for the reputation alone
Against: Something of a beast to drive, you'll probably never find one for sale
Verdict: It helps to be unhinged when it comes to driving one
Price Guide
Impossible to quote
Current Maker: None

Brutal is the only way to describe the amazing Zeta, which was basically an EM expanded by six inches in length with a Ford Zephyr 2.6-litre straight six engine shoehorned in. Tuned versions of up to 150bhp were offered! Suspension came from the TR3 and the nose looked different (with twin front intakes). Kits were expensive at £734 (or £868 with the 150bhp conversion) but the cars were very quick (120mph and 0-60mph in 7.8 secs) - not for the faint-hearted. One Zeta had a TR2 engine, and out of a mere five examples built over a four-year period, only three cars survive.

Fairthorpe Rockette

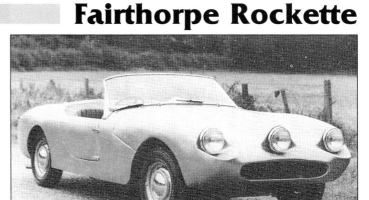

☆☆☆

Prod Years: 1962-67
Prod Numbers: Very few
For: Vitesse engine gives oomph (but low gearing makes a nonsense of long-distance travel)
Against: Standards of build were never very great, poorly thought-through details, much heavier than an EM so road behaviour suffers
Verdict: Less terrifying than a Zeta
Price Guide
More than an EM
Current Maker: None

While the EM relied on Spitfire engines, the Rockette used the lusty six-cylinder Vitesse in a body that was four inches longer than the EM. It also had a modified Electron nose with a cancerous extra central headlamp in it! Only three such bonnets were ever made, however: others got more conventional treatment, but one identification feature is that all Rockette bonnets had a bulge in them (later ones got two). The car used Triumph suspension with solid rear axle (or optional IRS). Most had removable side screens; some had sliding perspex windows in frames.

Fairthorpe TX-GT

☆☆☆

Prod Years: 1967-68
Prod Numbers: 7
For: Performance, handling, rust-free body, nothing else looks like it
Against: It's obvious why nothing else looks like it, build quality not very high, check for rust in the chassis
Verdict: Strange fish from an era when British specialist sports cars were everywhere
Price Guide
A £4500   **B** £3000   **C** £1800
Current Maker: None

Founder Donald Bennett's son Torix began to assert his own engineering genius and immediately made an impression by designing a new independent rear suspension system operated by transverse rods. The TX-1 prototype appeared in 1965 as an open car but made production as the TX-GT coupe from 1967, although sometimes with Triumph GT6 rear suspension (the complete GT6 chassis was used). Strange glassfibre body initially had no rear three-quarter windows, although small windows were soon added. 1968 GT MkII upped power from 95bhp to 104bhp, sufficient for a top speed of 112mph and 0-60 in 9.5 secs. Ousted by the TX-S and TX-SS.

Fairthorpe TX-S/TX-SS

☆☆☆

Prod Years: 1968-76
Prod Numbers: 4/6
For: Better handling than a GT6, highly individualistic character, great performance potential, rarity value
Against: Some very odd styling quirks, crudely put together, finding one might be a problem
Verdict: True British eccentric
Price Guide
A £4500   **B** £3000   **C** £1800
Current Maker: None

In 1968, Torix Bennett launched the new TX-S and TX-SS, which differed from the TX-GT by their larger rear quarter windows, fixed MGB GT rear screen and lower profile. The standard offering in the TX-S was an uprated 112bhp 2.0-litre Triumph GT6 engine, while the TX-SS boasted a 2.5-litre fuel-injected TR6 engine, which necessitated a hump in the bonnet and delivered up to 152bhp - enough for 130mph and 0-60 in 7.4 secs. Torix's transverse rod suspension was dropped after 1971, and a Triumph 1300 engine was also offered in the TX-S. But these could hardly be called popular Fairthorpes.

Falcon Competition

Ex-Ashley man Peter Pellandine set up Falcon Shells at Waltham Abbey, Essex, in 1957 to produce a duplicate Ashley bodyshell. The Competition was the company's first true kit car, although it was born as an extremely cheap (£65) shell for track use, though road versions became very popular. The curvy two-seater body could have optional and extremely evocative D-Type style twin head fairings. Engine options included Ford 105E/109E, Coventry-Climax and MGA. Complete kits, less engine and gearbox, cost £450. This is one of the more interesting specials era kits and worth looking our for.

Prod Years: 1958-63
Prod Numbers: Several hundred
For: Pretty bodywork (especially so with D-Type style head fairings), light weight, increasing cred in classic sports car circles
Against: Extremely basic, minimal weather protection
Verdict: How to look like Stirling Moss for very little outlay
Price Guide
A £4000   **B** £2200   **C** £800
Current Maker: None

Falcon Caribbean

The Caribbean was a stalwart sports car available in both open and closed forms. Mechanically it harked back to its specials era origins, using Ford 10 parts (and often Ford 10 chassis); however, alternative chassis were available, such as the LMB ladder chassis and Len Terry's specially designed tubular steel chassis (only a handful were thus fitted, however). Bodies cost from £115 and chassis from £50. From 1961, complete kits were offered, including new 105E or 109E engines, from £750, and front disc brakes became optional, as well as IFS and MGA/Climax engines.

Prod Years: 1957-63
Prod Numbers: Approx 500
For: Better looking than most glassfibre cars of this period, one with its own chassis is worth tracking down, can be made to go very quickly
Against: It goes like a pre-war Ford, don't expect it to be the least bit comfortable or refined
Verdict: Popular and now semi-classic
Price Guide
A £2500   **B** £1300   **C** £500
Current Maker: None

Falcon Bermuda

In response to public demand for a four-seater Falcon, the Bermuda was launched in January 1961, shortly before Peter Pellandine sold Falcon Shells (it became Falcon Cars Ltd and switched from its original Waltham Abbey base to a new factory in Hatfield, Herts). The rather unattractive Bermuda was essentially a Caribbean with a more squared-up hardtop and seating for four (although this was a rather optimistic promulgation). The same Ford 10 mechanical basis remained, so don't raise your hopes that this is a sports car.

Prod Years: 1961-63
Prod Numbers: Approx 200
For: Same plus points as the Caribbean with the added bonus of seating in the rear for small children
Against: There really isn't much space in the back and it looks far uglier as a result
Verdict: A less attractive package than the Caribbean
Price Guide
A £1500   **B** £1000   **C** £400
Current Maker: None

Falcon 515

Probably the most mature product of the specials bodyshell boom of the early 1960s was Falcon Cars' 515. A very handsome, almost Ferrari-like glassfibre body styled by Brazilian Tom Rohonyi was bonded to a multi-tubular spaceframe chassis. Mechanicals were taken from the brand new Ford Cortina (including its 1500cc 64bhp engine); the front end was independent and the rear axle was live. The 515 was intended to be a fully-built car, although many ended up being supplied in kit form. Only four cars are known to survive and it is believed that not a single one is actually on the road.

Prod Years: 1963-64
Prod Numbers: Approx 25
For: All-time great styling, reliable and effective Cortina mechanics, well made, lots of classic credibility
Against: Impossible to find for sale
Verdict: Sadly, a lost cause
Price Guide
Probably between £2000 and £5000
Current Maker: None

Falcon Sports

☆☆

Prod Years: 1984-date
Prod Numbers: Approx 200
For: Cheap and simple mechanicals, balanced appearance, actually a lot of fun to drive
Against: Potential rust in floorpan, crude in the extreme, performance doesn't match looks
Verdict: Less of a 'Sports' car, more of a fun machine
Price Guide
A £2500   **B** £1600   **C** £700
Current Maker: The 2CV Centre, Frome, Somerset

Peter Bird's name was already familiar when he launched the Falcon, since he had co-created the Stevens Cipher and helped develop the Lomax. Quite at odds with the Falcon's Lotus 7 style appearance, he elected to use the Citroen 2CV/Dyane/Ami floorpan. The simple body was a plywood-and-aluminium sandwich (which could also be built from a set of plans), so the price was kept to an absolute minimum (£406 all-in to begin with). There were glassfibre wings, the front ones being either flowing or cycle type. From 1993 made by The 2CV Centre, run by Mike Cooper, kit prices being from £2200 upwards.

Falcon LX3

☆☆☆

Prod Years: 1986-date
Prod Numbers: Included above
For: Zany zippiness, cheapy chirpiness, frolicking fun factor, lightweight laughs
Against: Morgan/Lotus 7 cross-over is peculiar, 2CV engine lacks power
Verdict: Much better than you might imagine
Price Guide
A £2500   **B** £1600   **C** £700
Current Maker: The 2CV Centre, Frome, Somerset

Alongside the four-wheeler model, Falcon launched the three-wheeled LX3 in 1986 as a direct competitor for the Lomax. It even had a very similar boat-tail rear end made of glassfibre, although it could hinge up for access, unlike the Lomax. Also different was its rear suspension: a new Falcon beam with a Citroen arm attached, and both sides of the Citroen suspension bolted to the beam. Same method of construction as the four-wheeler and same choice of cycle or flowing front wings. Kits cost £400 initially, rising as the years passed. Alternatively you could buy a set of plans for just £10.

Fletcher GT

☆☆☆☆

Prod Years: 1967
Prod Numbers: 4
For: Unusual style, all Mini bits, very well made, 2+2 seating
Against: Mini floorpan does rust, bonded-on body makes restoration difficult, extremely rare and expensive
Verdict: Interesting Ogle based spin-off
Price Guide
A £5000   **B** £2800   **C** £1400
Current Maker: None

Ogle made a fully-built car called the SX1000 between 1961-63, and they left behind a couple of interesting prototypes, one with a modified front and another with a modified rear. Boat-building company Norman Fletcher acquired the Ogle moulds and used both new designs to make one, updated GT. The nose featured a new inset headlamp arrangement behind perspex cowls, while the tail had a new sharp bustle and different light clusters. Whether all this was prettier than an original SX1000 is a moot point, but Fletcher returned to boat-making anyway.

Foers Nomad

☆☆☆☆

Prod Years: 1977-date
Prod Numbers: Approx 200
For: Tough construction, aluminium body panels, simple mechanicals, extremely versatile layout
Against: Rather basic and not what you'd call very pretty
Verdict: A great, individualistic modern, non rusting Mini Moke
Price Guide
A £2500   **B** £1200   **C** £600
Current Maker: Del Tech, Rotherham

The Nomad gets four stars because, for what it was, it was an excellent design. The kit car press 'discovered' it in 1981, but by then, from his workshop in Rotherham, John Foers had already made some 28 cars from as early as 1977. Unusually for a kit car, it had an all-aluminium body, mounted on a steel chassis. Into this structure went the subframes and mechanical components of a Mini. Body styles included a basic pick-up, a convertible (with optional doors), and a van/estate (which had an integral hardtop with a side-hinged rear door). The project was sold on to nearby Del Tech Ltd in 1990, and was kept low key, as ever.

Foers Triton

Wishing to update the Nomad concept, and to make it more civilised in the process, John Foers developed the Triton in 1985. The main difference was the employment of Metro subframes and mechanicals. Styling was a little sleeker, though still with flat glass all round, and the method of construction was identical: folded aluminium body panels over a perimeter frame, mounted on a tubular steel chassis. Only one body style: a three-door estate (or van) which boasted very large rear side windows. It never got the same push as the Nomad and was pensioned off to Del Tech along with its sister model in 1990.

Prod Years: 1985-date
Prod Numbers: Quite a few
For: Rugged construction, durable, rust-free body panels, smoother looking than Nomad, Metro parts are cheap and simple
Against: Still not very sophisticated
Verdict: Yorkshire farmers loved it
Price Guide
A £2700   **B** £1300   **C** £700
Current Maker: Del Tech, Rotherham

Futura

The first Futura was built in 1970 at the workshop of Robin Statham, whose company Fellpoint Ltd made the Minijem (qv). A humble VW floorpan lay underneath an incredible wedge-shaped body, whose windscreen hinged up sideways to allow the passengers to enter by climbing over the nose. Dashboard therefore to the right and four headlamps positioned (illegally) behind the screen, so pop-up units were developed. The money required to develop it eventually sank Fellpoint in 1971 and the prototype was cut up and exported to Brazil, but two Futura bodies were moulded at a later stage, one of which reached the road in 1979.

Prod Years: 1971
Prod Numbers: 3
For: Amazing wedge shape, novel windscreen-cum-door, extreme rarity value
Against: Darned impractical, windscreen sealing concerns, VW floorpan not really in character, not exactly bundles to choose from
Verdict: Fascinating curiosity of the exotikit era
Price Guide
Impossible to fix, but not expensive
Current Maker: None

Gazelle

Classic Motor Carriages of Florida, USA, has a lot to answer for: as early as 1975 it developed for the VW Beetle floorpan a plastic body which was vaguely reminiscent of the 1929 Mercedes-Benz SSK. Even stylist Dennis Adams was involved at one point. It first came to Britain in 1979 as an import priced at £15,000. Were there any takers? Does glassfibre make you hallucinate? Since then, it reappeared as the Amica, Delta, Spirit SS, Osprey, Gatsby and Phoenix, each having a shorter lifespan than the average mayfly. Some had front-mounted Cortina engines as an option to the Beetle. Slowly it sank in that no-one here bought them.

Prod Years: 1975-date (in USA)
Prod Numbers: Several thousand in USA, very few in Britain
For: Swank on a shoestring
Against: Silly proportions, Mercedes-Benz were right into rear-mounted flat-four engines in the 1930s
Verdict: Glitzy excrescence which should be melted down and used to make plastic coke bottles
Price Guide
A £3000   **B** £1750   **C** £900
Current Maker: None (in UK)

Gecko

Tamworth-based Nick Ingram of Autobarn Fabrications was behind the engaging little Gecko, a sort of modern Mini Moke. Inevitably, this meant it was based on Mini subframes and mechanicals, although Autobarn offered a good optional alternative to rusty rear subframes: a special beam axle with coil/over dampers. Steel box-section chassis frame, 1/2in plywood floor, aluminium body panels and glassfibre bonnet. Wheelbases varied from 50in to 100in, while a six-wheeled version was also offered. Upper bodywork was left free, and many owners did their own thing. Project passed in 1990 to Simmons Design of Lichfield.

Prod Years: 1984-92
Prod Numbers: Quite a few
For: Tough construction, high ground clearance, adaptable layout, jump-in-and-go spirit, cheap to buy and run, smarter than your average Moke kit
Against: Pretty basic, final competence dependent on builder's skills
Verdict: Utilitarian antidote to boredom
Price Guide
A £2300   **B** £1200   **C** £500
Current Maker: None

Gentry

☆☆☆☆☆

Prod Years: 1973-date
Prod Numbers: Approx 2000
For: Good-looking 'copy', usually reasonable quality
Against: Triumph chassis prone to rust, widely varying levels of build
Verdict: Established and trusty member of the kit car breed
Price Guide
A £4500   **B** £2500   **C** £900
Current Maker: SP Motors, Barwell, Leics

Alongside Jim McIntyre (maker of the Spartan), Roger Blockley's RMB Motors was first off the block to make an MG TF style car, in 1973. As he used to work on the Triumph Spitfire production line, basing the Gentry on a Herald/Vitesse chassis was natural. A tubular frame carried plywood inner body panels and aluminium main panels, plus GRP scuttle, wings and doors (and a cast replica of the MG Magnette ZA grille!). Spitfire version from 1975, or RMB's own chassis. Project passed to SP Motors in 1989, who developed a Ford-based chassis option. Two-seater or 2+2 versions and wide choice of degrees of completion.

Gilbern GT

☆☆☆☆☆

Prod Years: 1959-63
Prod Numbers: 15
For: Good performer, high quality of manufacture, four seats, practical mechanicals
Against: Pretty plain, not a brilliant chassis, Sprite engine feeble
Verdict: An established classic with a strong following
Price Guide
A £4000   **B** £2500   **C** £1600
Current Maker: None

Llantwit Major may not have the ring of a Maranello or Detroit, but for a while it was the car manufacturing capital of Wales. Formed by butcher Giles Smith and German-born Bernard Friese (hence 'Gilbern'). The Gilbern GT was a rather plain 2 + 2 coupe with a tubular steel chassis and glassfibre body. Front suspension derived from the Austin A35, rear axle was BMC and the gearbox came from MG. Engines ranged from the 948cc Sprite (optionally supercharged), to the 1098cc Coventry-Climax and MGA. It was good value and of high quality, and with an MG engine fitted, it could do a genuine 100mph.

Gilbern 1800GT

☆☆☆☆☆

Prod Years: 1963-67
Prod Numbers: 151
For: Solidly built, all proprietary MG parts, strong club and specialist following, classic credentials high
Against: Not the prettiest sports car around, nor the most sophisticated
Verdict: Underrated and quite collectable sports GT car
Price Guide
A £4000   **B** £2500   **C** £1600
Current Maker: None

At the 1963 Racing Car Show, the new 1798cc MGB engine became standard for the Gilbern GT and the revised model was renamed the 1800GT. It wasn't just the engine which was new: the front suspension was MGB and the MGB live rear axle was located by Panhard rod, and the brakes were MGB too. As it was lighter than the MG, Gilbern claimed 104mph and 0-60mph in 13.5 seconds, all for just £945. Tuning the engine produced an admirable GT car which attracted a burgeoning clientele: production increased substantially with this model.

Gilbern Genie

☆☆☆☆☆

Prod Years: 1966-69
Prod Numbers: 174
For: Lovely quality, pleasingly rapid, decent handling, nicely trimmed
Against: Hard ride, whippy chassis, rather heavy to drive
Verdict: Another excellent British sports car classic
Price Guide
A £6000   **B** £4000   **C** £2000
Current Maker: None

Smarter clothes for a strengthened version of the existing GT chassis made the Genie a good-looking grand tourer, moving Welsh manufacturer Gilbern firmly up-market. Engines were V6 units from Ford (2.5 or 3.0 litres, some with fuel injection), and up to 120mph was possible with the most powerful engine. However, there was rather too much power for the chassis, which tended to flex too much for comfort. Much of the MGB mechanical stuff remained, such as suspension, the rear axle and rack-and-pinion steering. All Genies came with twin fuel tanks and front disc brakes.

Gilbern Invader MkI/II

☆☆☆☆☆

The extremely handsome basic appearance of the Genie's GRP body was kept for Welsh manufacturer Gilbern's new 1969 Invader, but its chassis problems were addressed with a much stiffer design and improved suspension. Recognise an Invader MkI/MkII by its flush door handles (the Genie had Rover handles). 3-litre Ford V6 engine developed 144bhp. Dual overdrive was standard and an automatic box optional. Invader's cabin was more luxurious than previous Genie. MkII differs only in detail, and was also available as an estate (see below).

Prod Years: 1969-72
Prod Numbers: 74/187 (saloons)
For: Better handling than Genie, same attractions of smart style, fairly plush interiors, high build quality
Against: Never very sophisticated or refined compared to mainstream grand tourers
Verdict: A recognised gem
Price Guide
A £6000 **B** £4000 **C** £2500
Current Maker: None

Gilbern Invader Estate

☆☆☆☆☆

The attractive estate version of the Invader was marketed only in MkII form for a comparatively short time (1971-72), and hence is nowadays something of a rarity. It was actually first shown at the October 1970 Motor Show, though it took a while for it to enter production. Styling was natural, and it was a more convincing sports/estate than the Volvo 1800ES. These days, it is all but forgotten in favour of Scimitar GTEs - unfairly so, but understandable given its rarity. Good-looking and the perfect answer for the sports car enthusiast who refuses to have a vasectomy.

Prod Years: 1971-72
Prod Numbers: 105
For: Even more handsome as an estate, all the virtues of the saloon (easy mechanical parts, decent handling, well made)
Against: Very rare, some parts may now pose problems (though there's a very active club)
Verdict: Better than a Scimitar GTE
Price Guide
A £6000 **B** £4000 **C** £2500
Current Maker: None

Gilbern Invader MkIII

☆☆☆☆☆☆

Launched at the 1972 London Motor Show, the MkIII Invader was the ultimate and most sophisticated Gilbern. It was not really available in kit form, but is included here for completeness. Its suspension was upgraded to Cortina at the front (with adjustable dampers all round) and a Taunus live rear axle, plus accompanying changes to the chassis. Bodyshell was much modified: lower, with flared arches, revised rear end and wider front grille. Expect 125mph and 0-60mph in 7.2 seconds. Gilbern died in the oil crises years. Attempts were made to revive the famous Welsh company but all failed.

Prod Years: 1972-74
Prod Numbers: 195
For: Most sophisticated chassis and suspension set-up of any Gilbern, surprising ride, healthy performance, plush trim, good value
Against: Not that easy to find
Verdict: An excellent classic choice
Price Guide
A £6500 **B** £4200 **C** £2500
Current Maker: None

Ginetta G2

☆☆☆

After an early prototype which was destroyed, the Walklett brothers' first commercially available design was the 1958 G2, a car very much in the Lotus Six/Seven vein. Indeed it looked near-identical to the Lotus MkVI. It had a steel tube space frame chassis to which the very basic aluminium bodywork was fixed. It was intended for Ford sidevalve mechanicals, but a split axle independent front end conversion was available if required. Otherwise you could keep things very simple and cheap - kits cost just £156, so a fully-built car could be made for under £250. A popular machine in its day and nowadays very collectable.

Prod Years: 1958-60
Prod Numbers: Approx 100
For: Spindly looks, fundamentally 'right' space frame chassis, simplicity, fun factor, 'first of the line' kudos
Against: Ancient mechanicals, extreme crudity
Verdict: Lotus Six lookalike that makes its own statement
Price Guide
A £10,000 **B** £7000 **C** £4000
Current Maker: None

Ginetta G3

☆☆☆

Prod Years: 1960-62
Prod Numbers: Approx 60
For: Better body than most specials era shells, proven space frame chassis, very simple mechanically, more practical than a G2
Against: Not what you'd call handsome, still a very basic sports car, very hard to find
Verdict: Superior specials era product
Price Guide
A £7000 **B** £4000 **C** £2500
Current Maker: None

Late in 1960 arrived the Ginetta G3 which took the G2 chassis and clothed it in a modern-looking glassfibre shell. However, modern did not necessarily mean pretty, but at least you got ready-made inner wheel arches and boot floor (unlike many GRP shells of that era). Most G3s were sold as fixed-head coupes, but some open sports examples were also made. The usual Ford 100E sidevalve engine powered it. Pandering to the low-budget realities of most sports car enthusiasts, Ginetta also sold the G3 as a basic bodyshell under the name Fairlite. Today, a G3 is a real rarity.

Ginetta G4 Series I

☆☆☆☆☆☆

Prod Years: 1961-63
Prod Numbers: Approx 200
For: Fabulous handling for its era, very light, high performance potential, gorgeous lines, brilliant chassis
Against: Very basic, noisy and unrefined, expensive too
Verdict: Popular as a historic racer - and a genuine classic
Price Guide
A £15,000 **B** £10,000 **C** £7000
Current Maker: None

The G4 is the classic Ginetta, and the first volume-selling car the four Walklett brothers built. An attractive glassfibre body was bonded and bolted to a multi tubular space frame, initially with front coil springs and double wishbones, and the live rear axle was located by trailing arms and an A bracket. Optional front discs. Power came from the Ford 105E (997cc) Anglia engine, which was at least highly tunable. Kits were sold in complete form for £499. A Series I G4 is likely to be an open car (though a hardtop was offered) and will usually be used for historic racing, at which it is rather good.

Ginetta G4 Series II

☆☆☆☆☆

Prod Years: 1963-66
Prod Numbers: Approx 300
For: A little more practical than the S1, with a Cortina 1500 engine fitted it really flies, prettier rear end than S1
Against: What you'd expect really - hard, crude, cramped
Verdict: Extremely sought-after
Price Guide
A £13,000 **B** £8000 **C** £5500
Current Maker: Ginetta Cars, Sheffield

The distinctive Lotus MkVIII style finned rear wings of the G4 Series I were flattened out with the 1963 Series II, and also lengthened by some eight inches. That also allowed much more room for luggage. The Walkletts even gave you carpets in the standard kit! The Ford rear axle was ditched in favour of a BMC unit and a 1500cc Ford Cortina GT engine was a common fitment. In a car weighing under 1000lb, this was enough for 115mph and 0-50mph in 7 seconds. There was an optional hardtop (see pic), all-round discs and IRS. Revived in 1989 by Ginetta, mainly for the Japanese market. Beware of fakes.

Ginetta G4 Series III

☆☆☆☆☆

Prod Years: 1966-69
Prod Numbers: Approx 50
For: Much more refined than earlier G4s, pop-up lamp bonnet looks very attractive, usual handling/performance virtues, strong following
Against: Not as sought-after as previous G4 incarnations
Verdict: The perfect car for competitive and enjoyable historics
Price Guide
A £12,000 **B** £7000 **C** £4000
Current Maker: None

Major changes marked the introduction of the 1966 G4 Series III. An all-new square-tube space frame chassis was much stiffer than before and was designed to accept Triumph Herald front wishbones. The bodywork was revised too, particularly the bonnet which now incorporated pop-up headlamps and bumpers, and the windscreen, which was more sharply raked than before. Overall it was much more refined. A Cortina 1600 engine was offered later, but the G4 had passed its heyday. It was revived, however, in 1981 in Series IV form – a very different beast (see next page).

Ginetta G4 Series IV

Ginetta surprised everyone when it revived its classic G4 in time for the '80s boom in kit car sales. However, it was a thoroughly overhauled and much improved car: compared to the S3, it was 3in longer and 2in wider, had a bigger cockpit and boot, the windscreen gained a large surround, there was a roll-over bar and headlamps were fixed. The tubular spaceframe chassis was all-new, although very much based on the S3 type with its Triumph independent front suspension and Ford rear end. Standard engine was Ford's 1600 crossflow, with 1300 and 2000 options.

Prod Years: 1981-85
Prod Numbers: Quite a few
For: Scintillating magic of the G4 not lost, far more practical than a '60s G4, very useable and enjoyable
Against: For its era, still extremely basic and unsophisticated
Verdict: Pure-bred classic Ginetta - hunt one out now!
Price Guide
A £6000　　**B** £4000　　**C** £2000
Current Maker: None

Ginetta G10

With an eye on the American market, Ginetta developed a TVR Griffith style sports car to be powered by Ford's 4.7-litre V8 engine. There was a new space frame chassis clothed with a smooth glassfibre body which incorporated MGB doors and, on the convertible, an MGB screen. You got independent suspension by coil springs and double wishbones, and a four-speed Ford 'box. Not eligible for SCCA racing in the USA, so few were sold. In fact, there were only four G10 coupes, and two convertibles. Four went to the USA, and therefore your chances of finding a G10 for sale are, for all intents and purposes, zero.

Prod Years: 1964-65
Prod Numbers: 6
For: 150mph Cobra-eater, great image, very attractive shape, rarity
Against: Still rather crudely made, you're unlikely to find one for sale
Verdict: Like hens' teeth, and much sought-after in Ginetta circles
Price Guide
Impossible to quote, but expensive
Current Maker: None

Ginetta G11

Ginetta moved the original monster G10 more towards its MGB origins with the 1966 G11, in an attempt to garner home-market sales. In this it was unsuccessful, but only because BMC refused to supply Ginetta with the MGB doors and windscreens it needed to make it. 1800cc MGB engine, gearbox and rear axle (located by an A-frame and radius arms, suspended on coil springs). Complete kits cost only £1200, a real bargain considering that an MGB cost around £900 at the time. Ginetta made only two G11 coupes, the remaining ten being convertibles.

Prod Years: 1966
Prod Numbers: 12
For: Much prettier and more desirable than an MGB, and better all-round, great performance and road manners
Against: You'll have extreme trouble tracking one down, dowdy MGB mechanicals
Verdict: A true lost cause
Price Guide
Impossible to quote, but expensive
Current Maker: None

Ginetta G15

The G15 took Ginetta to a new level of importance in the specialist car industry. Its formula of low price, small dimensions and keen road manners struck a chord with British buyers. Glassfibre body was bonded to a square tube ladder frame, front suspension/disc brakes were Herald-derived and the trailing rear suspension, 875cc engine and transaxle came as one from the Sunbeam Imp Sport. 55bhp engine meant 95mph and high economy. Within months, a Series II version was introduced with a front-mounted radiator, Series III ('73) had improved trim, alloy wheels and larger rear quarter windows.

Prod Years: 1967-73
Prod Numbers: 580
For: Pretty shape, low centre of gravity gives sharp handling, cheap to run, good image, credible racer
Against: Bonded body makes restoration awkward, deserves more power
Verdict: Deservedly highly regarded as a sports car classic
Price Guide
A £6000　　**B** £4000　　**C** £2200
Current Maker: None

Ginetta G21

★★★☆☆

Prod Years: 1971-78
Prod Numbers: 68
For: Neat looking design, usual Ginetta handling finesse, can perform well (130mph with Ford V6)
Against: Only two seats, no boot lid, crude in too many ways
Verdict: Interesting and capable true specialist sports car
Price Guide
A £7000   B £4000   C £2500
Current Maker: None

Increasing maturity of design was evident in the G21, although it took a fair while to get it into actual production. A new backbone tubular steel chassis employed coil spring and wishbone front suspension and a subframe for the suspension and final drive at the back. Conceived to use Ford 3-litre V6 power and IRS, but in fact most were fitted with the 1725cc four-cylinder engine from the Sunbeam Rapier, also available in 95bhp G21S Holbay tune (plus a live rear axle). Not really a practical MGB rival. Not actually sold as a kit but included here for completeness. 1980s G23 and G24 developments never reached production.

Ginetta G25

★★★☆☆

Prod Years: 1983
Prod Numbers: 1
For: Clever use of Fiesta parts, handled and performed extremely well, usual Ginetta attention to engineering and quality
Against: Styling compromised by Fiesta doors/glass, never produced
Verdict: If this appeals to you, investigate a Ginetta G32
Price Guide
Not applicable
Current Maker: None

The G25 might seem a strange entry in this guide since it was never actually put into production. But it was offered for sale in kit form and is significant in Ginetta's history as it was its first mid-engined true road car. The design was based around Ford Fiesta doors, dash, seats and front and rear screens, and the complete Fiesta engine/'box slotted in behind the seats. Pop-up headlamps were a feature. Ginetta offered kits for sale but never made any more G25s, the model being redeveloped some years later into the fully-built G32.

Ginetta G26/G30

★★★★☆

Prod Years: 1984-92
Prod Numbers: Approx 280/10
For: Eminently practical, very high quality mouldings and engineering, excellent handling, spacious interior
Against: Styling compromised by Fiesta doors (which rust)
Verdict: The first kit car which was truly an alternative to mass-produced coupes
Price Guide
A £6000   B £3800   C £1750
Current Maker: None

Another new direction for the Walkletts: the G26 was a spacious four-seater coupe. Attractively styled and engineered, as ever, by Ivor Walklett, the G26 was the first to arrive (in 1984). It was designed to use a single Ford Cortina donor, the parts fitting in a strong steel chassis. The GRP body was cleverly designed around steel Fiesta doors and a Cortina windscreen. If a 2.8 or 3.0 V6 engine was fitted, you needed a restyled front end with fixed, rather than pop-up, headlamps, which was called the G30. The notchback G28 and G31 are described below. Planned Sierra IRS never materialised.

Ginetta G28/G31

★★★★☆

Prod Years: 1986-92
Prod Numbers: Approx 10/150
For: High quality mouldings, excellent chassis, proprietary Ford glass and engines, lighter than G26/G30
Against: They're an ugly pair compared to the long wheelbase cars (G28 is especially awkward), space in rear is cramped, styling has aged
Verdict: Effective '80s Ginetta coupes
Price Guide
A £6000   B £4000   C £2000
Current Maker: None

The original G26 was designed as a true four-seater, almost a saloon in fact. There remained a latent demand for a more overtly sporting coupe version, something of a successor to the G21 perhaps. As such, the Walkletts developed the G28 and G31 short-wheelbase notchback coupes which could seat 2+2, and they were first seen at the 1986 Motor Show. The G31 had the original pop-up lamp front end, while the G28 (as pictured, right) had the fixed headlamp nose and raised bonnet line intended for V6 engine installations. Chassis and running gear were unchanged from G26/G30.

Ginetta G27

The G27 was a developed version of the G4, immediately identifiable by its revised front end with pop-up headlamps. It had a space frame chassis, Triumph Vitesse based front suspension, Morris Ital or Escort rear axle (with IRS by wishbones and radius arms), shortened Jag driveshafts, usually Ford power (crossflow, Cosworth, V6 or Zetec), though other options included Mazda rotary, Fiat twin cam, Vauxhall 16-valve and Rover V8. Mark Walklett raced a rotary G27 very successfully. In 1995, its T-bar was removed, the front end was restyled and a pair of G33 inspired head fairings was added.

Prod Years: 1985-date
Prod Numbers: Approx 200
For: Great handling, low weight means lots of go, high quality, wonderful shape, good name
Against: Stark and unrefined in all respects, impractical
Verdict: One of the great jump-in-and-drive sports cars
Price Guide
A £9500 **B** £6000 **C** £3200
Current Maker: Ginetta Cars, Sheffield

GP Buggy

John Jobber was the man who brought Bruce Meyers' American dune buggy idea to Britain. In fact, it was a South African made buggy called the Lolette, a classic of the bath tub style. First ones were for shortened Beetle chassis, and they initiated a craze (GP were selling up to 100 kits a month). In the early days, many ex-agents offered rip-off GP shells which were of inferior quality or restyled their front and rear ends to create different models, many of which are described elsewhere in this book. Fill-out side panels and moulded screen surrounds were 1970s refinements. In 1992 the Buggies passed on to Ascot-based Roy Pierpoint.

Prod Years: 1968-date
Prod Numbers: Approx 4000
For: Kooky + wacky + yompy + grungy = buggy
Against: Old ones deteriorate rapidly, not exactly an all-weather machine, image a bit naff these days
Verdict: GP is the best name in buggies by far
Price Guide
A £3000 **B** £1600 **C** £600
Current Maker: GP Buggies, Amersham, Bucks

GP Super Buggy/Alpine

Offering a buggy on a standard, unshortened Beetle chassis was a logical move, since shortening was outlawed in some export markets. Thus the long wheelbase Super Buggy was born in 1970. Main advantage was a full four seats but other changes included a fluted front end and a more droopy rear. The Mk2 of 1975 gained proper moulded rear seats, wider wings and a new shape LDV-style main tub. Glassfibre screen surround and optional LDV/Ranchero bolt-on hardtops from 1977. 1979 Alpine got new side panels and wider, reshaped wings. Over 75% of production was exported, many kits going to Arab countries.

Prod Years: 1970-date
Prod Numbers: Approx 1500
For: Full four seats, one of the best-looking of all buggies, GP's name is synonymous with the best in buggies, still around
Against: Summertime car only, hardly practical even with four seats
Verdict: Buggies are making a comeback – can the world cope?
Price Guide
A £3000 **B** £1600 **C** £600
Current Maker: GP Buggies, Amersham, Bucks

GP Centron

As an insurance policy against the buggy boom going bang, GP developed the ungainly Centron, although this proved to be the damp squib, not the Buggies. It was the UK's first Beetle-based exotic kit car, a genre developed in the USA. Low glassfibre body for a VW floorpan. The distinctive flop-forward canopy (à la Bond Bug) used Austin Maxi dampers, but the whole thing leaked atrociously. Styling was by ex-Unipower man Val Dare-Bryan and GP's own Pierre du Plessis and looked rather like a sporting breadvan. At least it was distinctive. It proved to be a sales disaster (only 12 built), so dropped after one year. Five were exported.

Prod Years: 1970-71
Prod Numbers: 12
For: It's unusual and a very rare sight, Beetle bits are simple
Against: Not the last word in cool styling, canopy was a pain, rather underdeveloped
Verdict: It was a bit of a heap then, so you can imagine what they're like now
Price Guide
A £1200 **B** £800 **C** £400
Current Maker: None

GP LDV

☆☆☆☆☆

Prod Years: 1970-date
Prod Numbers: Approx 250
For: Novel approach, looks funky, if Del Trotter lived in Newhaven, he'd have one
Against: Pretty useless as a pick-up, getting in is a practised art
Verdict: The trendiest way to pick crabs up from the beach (that's crustaceans, not the result of illicit intercourse on the 'bed'...)
Price Guide
A £1200   **B** £800   **C** £400
Current Maker: GP Buggies

LDV stands for Light Delivery Vehicle, so the GP LDV was the ideal transporter for surf boarding establishments with a late shipment of Hot Tuna. It was based on the standard VW floorpan/Super Buggy. The short pick-up bed was wood-covered and could carry a nominal 10cwt. At first the reverse-angle hardtop was fixed, and incorporated Austin A40 rear glass as a windscreen. Later examples had removable hardtops, and doors were always optional - as was a rear seat conversion. Most LDVs went abroad, and there was licensed production elsewhere.

GP Ranchero

☆☆☆☆☆

Prod Years: 1974-date
Prod Numbers: Approx 150
For: You don't have to get wet or quite as draughty, semi-secure luggage space, kooky koncept
Against: Struggling to get in to the back seat (or the front seat come to that), trying to persuade anyone that this is remotely practical
Verdict: Can you believe it was described as a 'poor man's Reliant GTE'?
Price Guide
A £1500   **B** £800   **C** £400
Current Maker: GP Buggies

If you were a tripped-out, far-gone buggy case with contraceptive deficiency syndrome in 1974, then the Ranchero was there to comfort you. Yes, this was a four-seater estate buggy. Was this really supposed to be practical? Why, even the doors were optional, though you did get sliding perspex windows. Its fixed estate top used a hinged Austin A40 rear screen. Its public debut was at the 1975 Geneva Salon, no less! One or two van versions were made with panelled-in rear side bodywork. Eventually the Ranchero hardtop became a detachable option for the Super Buggy.

GP Centron II

☆☆☆☆☆

Prod Years: 1974-75/1983-87
Prod Numbers: Approx 4
For: More practical than the first Centron, unmodified Beetle chassis/greasy bits should make it easy to work on, it's rare
Against: Gawky styling compared to Nova and company, never properly finished, all but extinct
Verdict: Not so much a 'has been', more a 'never was'
Price Guide
A £1200   **B** £800   **C** £400
Current Maker: None

After a suitable gap following the semi-debacle of the first Centron (see previous page), GP tried again with a Centron II model in 1974. The Centron II had a revised rear end with a fixed rear window, Escort front screen and conventional opening doors. GP offered it at £995 plus tax but it never really entered production. Amazingly, it was revived in 1983 by new company Lalande, who made a grand total of two cars, and it was then revived again by MDB Sportscars, who renamed it the Sapphire. It was finally killed off in 1987, which was embarrassingly past its sell-by date.

GP Kübelwagen

☆☆☆☆☆

Prod Years: 1976-83
Prod Numbers: Approx 30
For: Great for turning up to WW2 re-enactments, more cred than a buggy
Against: By-standers sieg-heil you as you pass, pretty miserable as everyday transport
Verdict: Achtung! Diese Blitzkriegwagen ist verboten!
Price Guide
A £2000   **B** £1200   **C** £750
Current Maker: None

Siva founder Neville Trickett began his association with GP with the Kübelwagen. No prizes for guessing what this was a replica of, nor for the mechanical basis - an unshortened VW Beetle floorpan. Unlike the original, this had a glassfibre body, so there's no rust to worry about. Optional weather gear and various wartime appendages. I believe this was the first ever four-door kit car, though that's hardly a boast you're likely to share with your mates in the pub. GP also made the Camel, a third world 'modern' Kübel. You might also find Kübelwagen replicas made in the 1980s by GT Mouldings and by a chap called Steve Smith.

GP Talon

Neville Trickett went on to design the Talon for GP. The body was a sharply styled, rather Fiat X1/9-ish wedge in self-coloured glassfibre, and there was accommodation for 2+2 inside, but only just. The shame was the mechanicals: like all GP products up to that time, it used an unmodified VW Beetle floorpan. A novel feature was the gullwing doors, which could be removed for open-air motoring. Only 30 were made before a Mk2 revamp in 1983: this had a thicker rear pillar which freed up more space inside. By the 1980s, people's opinions of Beetle based kits were changing and GP sold out to Talon Sportscars.

Prod Years: 1979-92
Prod Numbers: Approx 150
For: Interesting styling, seating for four, good quality glassfibre
Against: Driving position, leaky doors, cramped interior on Mk1
Verdict: Get your claws into one for very little money
Price Guide
A £1700   **B** £1100   **C** £600
Current Maker: None

GP Madison

The next Trickett-styled GP was the one which gave GP its impetus in the 1980s. In fact this one was going to be sold by Trickett's own firm, Ground Effect Developments, but GP stepped in. The humorously styled body was influenced by Packard, and was highly individual. Underneath the GRP body sat, inevitably, a VW Beetle chassis (modified). However, the Madison was a natural for a front engine and GP took the plunge by launching a Cortina based chassis in 1983. Optional mohair hood and period parts. A company called OB&D tried to market Madisons with very up-market fittings and prices – with predictable results.

Prod Years: 1980-95
Prod Numbers: Approx 900
For: Swanky style, quality of mouldings, sense of humour, mechanical simplicity
Against: A bit gaudy for some, dynamics not a strong point, cramped
Verdict: Doing the Madison really is good for you
Price Guide
A £6000   **B** £3500   **C** £1700
Current Maker: None

GP Madison Coupe

If the Madison aped the Packard style, Neville Trickett's stunning Coupe version verged on the Bugatti-esque. The roofline was extremely low and the rear glass was tiny. Unlike the drop-top Madison, the Coupe had proper doors and even an opening boot. The kit was intended solely for the Ford Cortina based steel chassis. The glassfibre bodywork was self-coloured, and options included interior trim and softer springs. Like the Ford-based roadster, this model was taken on by a Kent firm called Madison Sportscar Company in 1989. Very few further examples were sold.

Prod Years: 1983-c92
Prod Numbers: 7
For: Alluring shape, wonderful aircraft-type doors, Ford mechanical basis, good quality mouldings
Against: Not for claustrophobes, very few around second-hand
Verdict: Belle epoque charm in abundance
Price Guide
A £6000   **B** £3500   **C** £2000
Current Maker: None

GP Spyder

GP's brilliant sales coup was to introduce a replica of the 718 RSK Porsche, so much more characterful than the rash of Speedsters around. Mr Trickett did the development work and the shortened VW chassis was - for once - totally authentic. Beautiful GRP replica body was extremely low (38in) and the level of accuracy was very high - there were instances of Porsche specialists being fooled, especially by the mid-engined Porsche-powered version (values double). Options included RS60-type windscreen and hood, and a special mid-mounted chassis for VW Golf engines (but few of these were sold).

Prod Years: 1982-date
Prod Numbers: Approx 1200
For: Brilliantly accurate reproduction, low centre of gravity means good handling, great GRP quality, high performance possibilities
Against: Awkward driving position, floorpans rust
Verdict: Superlative Porsche replica
Price Guide
A £8000   **B** £5000   **C** £2500
Current Maker: GP Developments, Princes Risborough, Bucks

Grantura Yak

★★★☆

Prod Years: 1970-73
Prod Numbers: Approx 150
For: All the advantages of the Moke (Carnaby Street cool, fresh-air fun, jump-in-and-go character), plus rust-free body
Against: All the disadvantages of a Moke (slow, draughty, noisy, leaky), plus dumpier styling
Verdict: Early Moke substitute
Price Guide
A £1000   **B** £500   **C** £200
Current Maker: None

Blackpool based Grantura Plastics had connections with TVR, and also made glassfibre hardtops for Mini Mokes. Hence it was not surprising that they should try a successor to the Moke when it left production in the UK in 1968. The Yak had a tubular chassis to which were bolted standard Mini subframes and a one-piece glassfibre body. It looked rather like a Moke, but had a Mini windscreen in a GRP surround and a longer rear overhang. Options included a full hood and a glassfibre hardtop. Grantura reckoned complete cars could be built for £400, and of the 150 cars built, some 30 were exported to sunnier climes.

Gravetti Cobra

★★☆☆

Prod Years: 1984-88
Prod Numbers: Approx 70
For: Should be cheap for a Cobra clone, ally-bodied one would be nice
Against: Moulding quality was poor, chassis needed work, authenticity was not meticulous
Verdict: Make sure you're not buying a lash-up – plenty are about
Price Guide
A £7500   **B** £5000   **C** £3000
Current Maker: None

This was a development of the AD Cobra replica, one of the early and rather unsatisfactory attempts (see page 11). In the early days, the Gravetti too was a particularly awful job. It was run by Nigel Gravett who operated from premises in Mere, Wiltshire. Various Ford bits were used underneath, and recommended engines included Ford V6, Rover V8 and Yank V8s. GRP body with steel inner frame, or all aluminium. Gravetti launched the catchy 'Cob in a box' idea: everything you need short of a power train. After Gravetti went bust, it was revived and the chassis re-engineered by Bob Egginton of ASD to become the CK 427 (qv).

Griffin/GDXM

★★★☆

Prod Years: 1975-85
Prod Numbers: Approx 20
For: Clever and adaptable concept, styling still looks modern
Against: Quality was never great, detail design integrity lacking, Minor/Beetle basis was silly
Verdict: Could have been a great car, but sadly it wasn't
Price Guide
A £1300   **B** £800   **C** £500
Current Maker: None

This is one of those cars falling into the 'if only' category. It had such promise: the styling was sharp and advanced, and the body concept was clever - you could lift the estate-type hardtop right off for open-topped motoring in fine weather. But the Poole-based company chose the wrong donor: the Morris Minor, whose mechanicals fitted into a tubular chassis of the firm's own design. Alternatively, from 1978 a VW floorpan could be used under a longer shell, but this was hardly any better. Launched as the GDXM, but the name quickly changed to Griffin. Despite attempts to develop it, it just faded quietly away from the scene.

Group Six

★★☆☆

Prod Years: 1972-77
Prod Numbers: Quite a few
For: Looks vaguely like a late 1960s Group 6 racer
Against: But it doesn't sound like one, go like one, or do anything like one come to that
Verdict: It was one of the shoddy kit cars of the 1970s, and surely most have long since been scrapped
Price Guide
A £1200   **B** £700   **C** £200
Current Maker: None

Londoner John Mitchell built the first Group Six in 1972, obviously inspired by the old Group 6 sports/racing style. Underneath the glassfibre body, however, lay nothing more exotic than a VW Beetle floorpan. The prototype had a Vauxhall Cresta windscreen, but production examples got Ford Capri glass, and other improvements on later cars included larger doors, angle iron body strengthening and the availablity of a targa hardtop from late 1973. Even later cars swapped their open bodywork for an enclosed coupe style. Dave Lee Travis drove one in the *Wonderful Radio One* film, but that was this car's sole claim to fame.

GRS Tora

☆☆☆☆☆

Few people were expecting Ginetta to turn their attention away from full-blooded sports cars to kit-built estates, but they did so in 1983. So different was it from the normal Ginetta product that the Walkletts formed a new marque to sell it: GRS. The Tora was also unique in using a Hillman Hunter as its donor, and it took just about everything from it: doors, windscreen, interior and of course all the mechanicals. The style was Matra Rancho, the chassis was a galvanised steel ladder frame, the bodywork glassfibre with a proper opening tail gate. Ginetta developed a four-door Cortina-based Tora 2 in 1989, then sold out.

Prod Years: 1983-89
Prod Numbers: Approx 350
For: Spacious interior, very solidly built, eminently practical, rust-free
Against: Rather boring, Hunter mechanicals not favoured
Verdict: So much better than a Dutton Sierra or Carlton Commando
Price Guide
A £2500   B £1400   C £500
Current Maker: None

GSM Delta

☆☆☆☆☆

This sports car was actually of South African origin, created by Bob van Niekirk and Vester de Witt, and built from 1958. The UK manufacturing operation began in 1960, but lasted less than a year. Steel tube ladder chassis with tuned Ford Anglia power (optional Coventry-Climax for racing), subframes carrying transverse leaf spring front suspension and 100E rear axle with coil springs. Bodywork: open or coupe, the latter having a reverse-angle rear screen. South African production continued until 1964 when the firm's ambitous plans over-reached themselves.

Prod Years: 1960-61 (in UK)
Prod Numbers: 35 (in UK)
For: Pretty shape, tunable Anglia engine, light weight (12cwt), eligible for historic competition
Against: Very hard to find, Z-back coupe is not a pretty sight
Verdict: Classic road/race cross-over
Price Guide
Too rare to quote, but probably £3-8000
Current Maker: None

GSM Delta Fastback

☆☆☆☆☆

The GSM Delta was designed by racing enthusiasts for racing enthusiasts, and there were lightweight racing versions as well as the very rare Fastback model. This had delightful fixed roof styling and the prototype's bodywork was fabricated by Williams & Pritchard in aluminium. It was quite possibly the cost of developing this model that forced UK production to end (in liquidation), and it is believed that only two Fastback models survived. The idea of a coupe GSM was revived in 1963, after Van Niekirk returned to South Africa, when a new model called the Flamingo was launched.

Prod Years: 1961
Prod Numbers: Tiny handful
For: Classic '60s sports car lines, aluminium bodywork, very light weight, great for racing
Against: Impractical, where would you look to find one?
Verdict: Attractive beast of near-mythical rarity
Price Guide
Too rare to quote, but more than ordinary Delta
Current Maker: None

GTM

☆☆☆☆☆

This amazingly long-lived two-seater kit car began life as the Cox GTM (Grand Touring Mini) in 1966. Mini front subframes were used front and rear, so that the engine was mid-mounted in a semi-monocoque steel structure and glassfibre body panels. Special rear suspension and gear linkage. It lasted little over a year before going to Howard Heerey in 1968, who made it more refined, for example adding a supporting frame for the engine in 1971. Made by GTM Cars from 1973, KMB Autosports from 1976 and Patrick Fitch and Peter Beck's GTM Cars from 1980 to 1995. Later developments included 12/13in wheels, an 'export' bonnet and optional flared wings.

Prod Years: 1966-date
Prod Numbers: Approx 500
For: Mid-engined handling balance, classic looks, Mini bits, light weight, good economy
Against: Rust in older chassis, cramped interior, not much luggage space
Verdict: Attractive and rewarding miniature Ferrari
Price Guide
A £4000   B £2000   C £800
Current Maker: Primo Designs, Stoulton, Worcs

Invader

Prod Years: 1971-79
Prod Numbers: Approx 150
For: Smoother body style than most buggies, a cut above the rest in quality terms too
Against: Likely to be pretty shabby by now, discomfort factor relegates it to summer use only
Verdict: Superior buggy, but difficult to get worked up about
Price Guide
A £1700   **B** £1000   **C** £500
Current Maker: None

The early fortunes of Jim Cullen's GB Motors were based on ripping off the GP Buggy, albeit slightly modified as the GB Buggy. The altogether more professional Invader buggy began life as an original looking American shell called the Scorpion, which was restyled by GB Motors for UK manufacture. Based on a shortened Beetle floorpan, complete kits were quite expensive for buggies, retailing at £250. A Mk2 Invader arrived in 1974, sporting a deeper main body tub and optional glassfibre windscreen surround and hardtop. Project passed to Croy of Birmingham in 1977, though production ground to a halt in 1979.

Jago Geep/Sandero

Prod Years: 1971-date
Prod Numbers: Approx 2000
For: Rugged nature, proven off-road ability, jeep looks, cheap Ford or Suzuki parts, tough chassis, lots of options
Against: Fairly basic and uncomfortable, avoid early examples
Verdict: Ride 'em rough shod
Price Guide
A £3200   **B** £1500   **C** £500
Current Maker: Jago Developments, Chichester

Geoff Jago was offering street rod kits as early as 1965, and branched out in 1971 to create the Geep. The glassfibre body was moulded directly off a genuine Willys Jeep and mounted on a simple ladder chassis designed for Ford Anglia 105E parts. Kits were cheap at £190 including hood and side screens. Morris Minor based version from '74, definitive Escort Mk1/2 based Geep from '76. Roll-cage introduced in 1984, much revised bodywork from 1987. The Geep name was dropped in 1991 (Chrysler wanted to sell Jeeps in the UK) and renamed Sandero. Suzuki 4x4 based version was launched in 1994.

Jago Samuri

Prod Years: 1983-90
Prod Numbers: Approx 130
For: Four seats, reasonable quality, simple mechanically, adaptable roof set-up, moulds still exist
Against: Utterly bizarre styling, leaky roof, not really very comfortable, Jago couldn't spell 'samurai'
Verdict: More sensible, 1980s-style beach buggy
Price Guide
A £1800   **B** £1100   **C** £500
Current Maker: None

When Jago launched the Samuri in 1983, it made a lot more sense than it does now. At the time, there were hardly any practical four-seater kits, and the Dutton Sierra was selling by the barn-load. The Samuri stepped in, offering generous dimensions, spacious four-seater interior, permanently fixed T-bar roof, lift-out roof panels, lift-off solid half-doors and a removable rear hard top. The styling was a weird kind of post-buggy/sports/estate fusion and definitely a matter of individual taste. All-GRP bodywork, steel box section chassis, Ford Escort mechanical parts. The Samuri dated very rapidly.

JBA Falcon

Prod Years: 1982-date
Prod Numbers: Approx 1000
For: Very high quality, lots of development work, good chassis, refined, spacious, excellent hood
Against: Rather upright styling
Verdict: Superlative quality and rightly one of the kit car industry's most highly regarded products
Price Guide
A £8000   **B** £5000   **C** £2000
Current Maker: JBA Engineering, Wigan

One of the trailblazers for an era of better quality kits, JBA created its Falcon in 1982. The bodywork was upright and traditional in style, and initially made of individual steel panels, though that changed to aluminium with GRP wings fairly quickly (all-GRP bodywork followed in due course). Steel ladder/perimeter frame chassis became a tubular cruciform in time. Ford Cortina Mk III/IV/V components (though optional Ford V6 power was also available). Hardtop offered from 1984, naturally a high-quality item. Proved to be immensely popular. Plus 2 version launched 1986 (see Volume 4). Never cheap, because it was built up to a quality.

JBA Javelin

The idea behind the Javelin was quite sound, even clever, but it never achieved much success. Although it was disguised quite well, the Javelin was basically a convertible glassfibre Ford Capri (below the waist it was all but identical). There was a steel chassis under it, fitted with Capri Mk2 mechanicals, interior, doors, lights and glass. The GRP bonnet was restyled to look like a Lagonda, while the roof was a novel convertible style, featuring a fixed targa bar and fold-down rear section. It was well-made - too well-made, in fact, since it was so labour-intensive to do that it became uneconomic to keep going.

Prod Years: 1985-89
Prod Numbers: Approx 50
For: Capri interior and many other parts, four full seats, well conceived targa top, excellent quality
Against: Capri doors rust, slightly naff image of modded Capri
Verdict: If you like Capris, this makes an unusual and attractive alternative
Price Guide
A £3500   **B** £2000   **C** £750
Current Maker: None

Jeffrey J4

Jeffrey Racing Cars of Oxfordshire built various Formula 750 racers from 1968 before customers asked for road cars. George Jeffrey built a prototype which he called J4 and gave it to a customer for evaluation, the feedback refining subsequent cars. Near racing-spec space frame chassis, Ford engines, Morris Minor or Cortina rear axle, Mini rack, Formula 750 suspension. Aluminium main body panels plus GRP wings, nose and bonnet. The J4 weighed only 10cwt, so performance potential was substantial. No two cars were identical, and many were raced as well as road-driven.

Prod Years: 1971-72
Prod Numbers: Approx 30
For: Racing chassis and suspension, light weight, faultless handling
Against: Hardest ride in history, no seat padding and exposed seating position, generally spartan air
Verdict: The nearest you'll get to a classic kit for the track
Price Guide
A £5000   **B** £3500   **C** £1500
Current Maker: None

Jeffrey J5

While the J4 was a racer with road bodywork, the replacement J5 (also known as the JS5) was more purpose designed for road use. Strengthened J4 chassis, softer suspension, Triumph Herald steering, but still Ford engines (1300 or 1600). The bodywork was much more curvaceous, at first built to the same aluminium-and-GRP spec as before, though from '73 an all-glassfibre body was employed. Easier to build, easier to live with, but still a driver's car in the best sense of the word. George Jeffrey tired of road cars and sold out to racing driver Dave Cox of Emba Cars, who made six further J5s from '74.

Prod Years: 1972-75
Prod Numbers: 32
For: More elegant and habitable than J4 but still a sharp handler and excellent performer
Against: Compared to most cars, it's still pretty basic
Verdict: One of the few credible alternatives to a Lotus 7 - it doesn't have the name, but it does have the ability
Price Guide
A £5500   **B** £3600   **C** £1600
Current Maker: None

Jiffy

Commercial vehicles are not generally speaking covered in this guide, but kit-form vans are rare beasts and the Jiffy deserves a mention because it was styled by one of the industry's greats, Richard Oakes. In response to the Honda Acty (the first Japanese micro-van to come to the UK), this was a Mini-based chassis/cab kit with a pretty little glassfibre cab; you added your own choice of pick-up, flat bed or van rear end. Kits cost £1150 and were manufactured by Mechanical Services of Bolton, Lancashire. In the end, commercial buyers did not want unwarranted kit-built vehicles, which remain almost unheard of.

Prod Years: 1982-c84
Prod Numbers: A few
For: Cute styling, rust-free body, cheap and everlasting Mini bits, good carrying abilities
Against: Not many were sold, it was all very much at the budget end of the market
Verdict: The perfect machine for transporting lemons on pancake day
Price Guide
A £1200   **B** £700   **C** £300
Current Maker: None

Jimi Jimp

Prod Years: 1981-84
Prod Numbers: A few
For: Well designed, honest, very tough, well built
Against: Extremely basic, hasn't got the 'cool' of a Moke, Reliant mechanicals aren't very sophisticated, only two seats
Verdict: If you don't have too high expectations, this could make a good little workhorse
Price Guide
A £1000   B £600   C £250
Current Maker: None

Peter Kukla ran a restoration business in Sandbach, Cheshire, and to fill his spare capacity he created the Jimi Jimp, which was styled by Steve Kirk. Not one curve was to be seen in this utility-type car, which used a Reliant Kitten van chassis and box section steel supporting frame. The steel inner body (clothed in aluminium panels) was simply riveted in place, and the bonnet hinged forward for access. Optional canvas tilt, roll-over bar and doors. Not many were sold, and those that were tended to go to Africa and the Caribbean in CKD form. The Jimp's fate was sealed when Reliant pulled the plug on the Kitten.

Jimini

Prod Years: 1973-83
Prod Numbers: Several hundred
For: Mokey benefits of fun, four seats and practicality, later ones don't look like just another Moke kit
Against: Avoid steel-bodied ones unless rust-proofed, usual Moke drawbacks of noise, draughts and hard ride
Verdict: For Mokers, the Jimini might not be cricket, but it's worth a look
Price Guide
A £2500   B £1250   C £500
Current Maker: None

The Mini Moke left production at Longbridge in 1968 and the kit car industry was not slow in producing alternatives. The first Jimini in 1973 not only looked very like the Moke, it was also unique in having an all-steel body, just like the Moke. However, the front end was distinctively restyled in 1976 around square headlamps, a sloping bonnet and a new grille. It was sold by a new company, but procution was rather sporadic, there being a number of gaps in production. The Jimini's body switched in 1983 to glassfibre monocoque, whereupon it was known as the Jimini 2 (see below).

Jimini 2

Prod Years: 1983-date
Prod Numbers: Approx 50
For: Mokey fun, Mini cheapness, almost totally rust-free, doesn't look like just another Moke kit
Against: GRP bodies must be prang-free, the front end is a matter of taste, it's all pretty basic and uncomfortable
Verdict: Buy Jimini
Price Guide
A £2500   B £1250   C £500
Current Maker: Scamp Motor Company, Crawley, Sussex

After a short gap in production of the all-metal Jimini described above, a glassfibre monocoque Jimini 2 was offered from 1983. Styling was smoothed out around the front end and a number of minor improvements were made. The windscreen was now taken from the Mini and fitted in a glassfibre surround. Again there were gaps in production but the Jimini 2 was definitively revived by the project's original instigator, Dave Cameron, for the 1990s. Arch rivals Scamp eventually took the Jimini over and added a Metro based option, and it's still available today.

Karma

Prod Years: 1982-date (in UK)
Prod Numbers: Approx 1000
For: Ferrari-ish looks, 2+2 seating, fairly simple mechanically
Against: Quality often lacking, Beetle based cars a let-down, some styling anomalies, may need a lot of fine tuning by the builder/owner, dynamically disappointing
Verdict: Left-over from the 1970s struggling to keep up-to-date
Price Guide
A £4500   B £2500   C £800
Current Maker: RW Kitcars, Leics

The Karma was first seen in the UK under the wing of Dave Perry's Automotive Developments as a US-made import. Moulds were taken in the UK and production started, but was almost immediately taken over by Roger Woolley's RW Kit Cars. The American Custom Classics Karma was a vague Ferrari Dino lookalike based on a Beetle floorpan. RW offered this but quickly added a replacement chassis option and, more significantly a front-engined chassis for Ford Cortina parts. There was also a mid-engined chassis for a wide variety of engines up to Rover V8, and a chassis with Jag running gear. Some nice examples were built but many were dogs.

Kestrel/Briton

★★★★☆

The Kestrel had a lot going for it: it was very well designed, looked quite pretty, and was made to top quality standards by Dorset-based Protoflight, an operation more usually involved with the aircraft industry. Its one problem was what lay underneath - a VW Beetle floorpan and four-pot banger in the boot. Peter Iredale was the designer, and he paid lots of attention to detail: box-section subframes front and rear, thick glassfibre body panels, special wiring loom, chromed brass windscreen, double-skinned doors. Project passed in 1988 to a Scottish firm called FES, which renamed the car the Briton.

Prod Years: 1984-89
Prod Numbers: A few
For: Top-flight mouldings, attractive design, good interior space, plenty of pleasing design details
Against: Depressing Beetle flat four exhaust note
Verdict: If you are sympathetic to the Beetle basis, this could be a great buy
Price Guide
A £2000   **B** £1200   **C** £700
Current Maker: None

Kestrel Scorpion

★★☆

When the kit car boom got going in the early 1980s, all sorts of prehistoric kits were revived. One of these was the Tom Killeen-designed Scorpion (see page 91), which was resurrected by Berkshire-based Peter Sylvester of Dovetail Plastics in 1984. The old car's rear-engined Imp basis was ditched and the semi-monocoque design totally overhauled. Now the company offered a space frame chassis with suspension which, it was claimed, had been developed in conjunction with Lotus. A mid-mounted Alfasud engine was specified. The GRP shell was much as before, now reinforced with Kevlar.

Prod Years: 1984-85
Prod Numbers: Very few
For: Unusual shape, Alfasud power
Against: Underdeveloped, gullwing doors and pop-up lamps never properly sorted, quality very poor, no-one ever tested one
Verdict: Perhaps it would have been better to let old dogs lie
Price Guide
A £1100   **B** £750   **C** £500
Current Maker: None

Kilo Sports

★★★★☆

What a strange fish the Kilo Sports was. Quite apart from its appearance - a trad-style roadster with breeze-block styling - the mechanical basis was, curiously, the Morris Minor 1000. It was designed by a Morris Minor specialist called David Stiff and built at The Thousand Workshop in Bodmin, Cornwall. Basic doorless glassfibre body, steel ladder chassis, one-piece front/rear wings, standard roll-over bar, BMC 1100/1300 radiator, Bedford HA van pedals, standard aero screens or optional full windscreen and hood. More performance could be achieved by fitting a 1275cc MG Midget engine. Briefly revived in 1986.

Prod Years: 1983-84/1986
Prod Numbers: Very few
For: Reliable Minor parts, actually quite fun to drive, well made
Against: Upright and weirdly sculpted body, cart spring rear suspension not really sporting, slow, no doors, pretty crude
Verdict: Doomed to obscurity - maybe of interest to broad-minded Morris Minor lovers?
Price Guide
A £1400   **B** £1000   **C** £400
Current Maker: None

Kingfisher Sprint

★★☆

Craft teacher Roger King was nothing if not ambitious. His raw material was basically not very promising (he was reviving the 1966 Minijem), but he planned to do battle with Porsche. The Minijem was substantially redesigned: 6in longer, 2in taller, and sporting a VW Beetle windscreen, Datsun 120Y Coupe rear screen, Ford Capri rear lights and big front and rear spoilers. Underneath the GRP bodywork were Mini parts, and King even offered a 1480cc Super Sports engine with a Rajay turbocharger - good for 125bhp! Sold complete as well as in kit form from premises in Northumberland. Revived in 1985 as the Vortex.

Prod Years: 1982-84/1985
Prod Numbers: A few
For: Updated Minijem styling, cheap Mini bits, usual good handling and performance of this sort of car
Against: Quality not too hot, no boot lid, lumpy design details not to everyone's liking
Verdict: Basically a bit of a sow's ear
Price Guide
A £1500   **B** £1000   **C** £500
Current Maker: None

Kingfisher Kombat

Prod Years: 1984-91
Prod Numbers: 42
For: Classic buggy pluses (fun, fun and more fun), and it's likely not to have deteriorated quite so much
Against: Classic buggy minuses (wind, rain and more wind and rain)
Verdict: If you must have a Vulture buggy, make it a Kombat
Price Guide
A £2500   **B** £1300   **C** £600
Current Maker: None

Volkswagen specialists and contracted buggy moulders Kingfisher Kustoms rediscovered the long-deceased Vulture buggy (see pg 111) in 1984 and decided to modify and relaunch it in the height of the UK's early '80s kit car boom, saying it "marks the beginning of a resurgence of interest in buggies". The VW 'pan needed to be shortened by 16 inches. The basic kit (at £475) included a centre console, screen, roll-over bar, side mouldings, seat shells and distinctive square headlamps. Kingfisher only withdrew the model when it decided to stop doing glassfibre work. The moulds still exist at Kingfisher, and there is some pressure from enthusiasts to re-enter production.

Kingfisher Kommando/Chenowth

Prod Years: 1983-date
Prod Numbers: Approx 70/100
For: As whacky as they come, very light weight means great performance, low centre of gravity helps handling, virtually indestructible
Against: Very very crude, no weather gear or trim, not really suited to road use
Verdict: Could turn you into a dune-seeking missile
Price Guide
A £4000   **B** £2000   **C** £1000
Current Maker: Kingfisher Kustoms, Smethwick, W Midlands

The American sand-rail idea achieved a brief flurry of popularity over here, but we're not really endowed with the right quantity of vast deserts for the sport to catch hold. Therefore most rails were bought because they looked outrageous. Kingfisher's one was better on and off road than the UVA Fugitive, but not as good as the legendary US-made Chenowth (which Kingfisher also imported). The recipe is familiar: an indestructible steel tube space frame housing VW suspensions and a Beetle engine out back and clothed with the simplest GRP body panels. Options included V6 and V8 engines and trick suspensions.

Kingfisher Kango

Prod Years: 1985-90 (in UK)
Prod Numbers: 12
For: Interesting shape, versatile packaging, option of full hard top or fresh air fun, standard Beetle bits
Against: It's still just a rebodied Beetle, scarce
Verdict: Connoisseur's sports buggy
Price Guide
A £3000   **B** £1700   **C** £900
Current Maker: None

This novel modernised buggy came from South Africa and was made in the UK by Dave Fisher's Kingfisher Kustoms. Designed to fit a full-length VW Beetle floorpan, the glassfibre body was smart and angular. It was also adaptable: the solid doors could be removed and replaced with soft doors, the rear coupe section incorporated a hatchback and it, too, could be removed and a lockable boot lid used instead. Only the large laminated central roll-over bar remained fixed. Some nice touches in evidence: strengthening box sections in the body and little moulded-in tubes to carry the wiring.

Kingfisher Mouldings Countess

Prod Years: 1982-86
Prod Numbers: Quite a few
For: It might have looked exotic in 1982 but nothing else!
Against: Just plain depressing: ripply bodyshell, awful styling, poorly thought-through engineering, many were left unfinished in people's gardens and allowed to rot
Verdict: The crappest Countach copy you will ever see
Price Guide
A £1200   **B** £900   **C** £400
Current Maker: None

Some people really look down their noses at kit cars, and abominations like the Countess are the main reason. Just about everything was wrong with it but, because it was the very first (albeit supremely feeble) attempt to offer something that looked like a Countach, quite a few were sold. The man responsible for it was Wigan-based Dave Forsyth. The standard offering was for a Beetle floorpan, though a multi-tube chassis was also designed to accept two Austin Maxi front subframes and Maxi engine, or a Rover V8. All were virtually unbuildable, as was the later, more accurate Countach shell (sold to GB).

Kougar Sports

☆☆☆☆☆

Fabulous is the only way to describe Rick Stevens' Kougar Sports, unusually based on Jaguar S-Type components, which fitted in a space frame chassis, along with an MGB steering rack, and a glassfibre body plonked on top. This had echoes of Frazer Nash and was designed for pure fun: therefore there were no doors, while the roll-over bar, windscreen and weather gear were optional. Kits were very expensive (over £3000 at launch in 1977), but ready trimmed and beautifully finished. In time, a Rover V8 power option became available. Taken over by Phil Street in 1990 and greatly improved, then new owners in 1994. Most went to the US.

Prod Years: 1977-date
Prod Numbers: Approx 230
For: Classic cigar shape, Jaguar donor parts just right, great performance (120mph, 0-60 in 6 secs), very high quality engineering
Against: Really only suited to fun use in good weather
Verdict: One of the purest and most enjoyable fun cars ever
Price Guide
A £12,000   **B** £8500   **C** £5000
Current Maker: Kougar Cars, Warwick

Kougar Monza

☆☆☆☆☆

Originally seen as early as 1980, the Monza was a vaguely Ferrari inspired sports car. Cortina power and a high price meant only seven of the original type were made. Attempted Mk2 resuscitation in 1984 with Rover V8 power, 1985 Mk2 (3 built) had V8/Jaguar power options. But the definitive Monza (Mk3) arrived in 1993 with Jaguar XJ6 underpinnings and power train. This did away with the vents behind the wheelarches. A full screen and weather gear were offered from 1993, but the project passed to new owners in 1994 and was re-engineered to accept American V8 engines in addition to the Jaguar units.

Prod Years: 1980-date
Prod Numbers: Approx 30
For: Wonderful shape, unstinting quality, finely developed chassis offering sharp handling
Against: Hard to find one, early ones had dynamically challenged Cortina parts (but only 7 were made)
Verdict: If you find one for sale, buy it or tell us about it
Price Guide
A £12,500   **B** £8000   **C** £4000
Current Maker: Kougar Cars, Warwick

KVA GT40 MkIII

☆☆☆☆☆

Ken Atwell began the GT40 replica craze, and he was in the right place to do so: employed by Ford, he was allowed to take a mould off a genuine MkIII GT40 kept at Swansea. That was in 1982, and soon he was persuaded to go into kit production. A tubular steel space frame was used, accepting Cortina MkIII/IV suspension and steering, VW gearbox and engines ranging from Ford CVH to Rover V8. The long-tail MkIII shell was not as popular as the race-style MkI, launched in 1984. KVA's kits were very difficult to build, so other firms (notably Tornado and GTD) did much better using KVA shells, although no-one really took up the MkIII shape.

Prod Years: 1982-92
Prod Numbers: A few
For: Authentic looking bodywork and interior, mould quality good
Against: Early ones were unsophisticated, build quality variable, avoid Ford-engined ones, the MkIII style body is not popular
Verdict: Pioneer of the GT40 world which got better as the years went by
Price Guide
A £18,000   **B** £12,000   **C** £7000
Current Maker: None

KVA GT40 MkI

☆☆☆☆☆

Ken Atwell quickly realised that the public wanted replicas of the classic Le Mans winning MkI GT40, not the watered-down long-tail MkIII which he had originally replicated. Therefore he produced a MkI shell in 1984, based around the Jacky Ickx winning GT40. KVA offered its usual rather basic body/chassis kit for £3500 and other firms were left to develop the idea further from a technical point of view, and to finish the replicas off properly (eg MCR Phoenix in the north, GT Developments in the south, and so on). The KVA MkI can be said to have truly begun the currently burgeoning GT40 replica scene.

Prod Years: 1984-92
Prod Numbers: Quite a few
For: Fine quality mouldings, firmly accurate visual reproduction, easily maintained proprietary mechanicals
Against: KVA cars were never 100% developed, beware of botched builds
Verdict: The original but sadly nowhere near the best
Price Guide
A £18,000   **B** £12,000   **C** £7000
Current Maker: None

Kyote

☆☆☆☆

Prod Years: 1971-76/1991-date
Prod Numbers: 45 (in UK)
For: Smart styling for a buggy, practicality greatly enhanced by doors and especially optional estate-type hardtop
Against: It's still basically an old Beetle underneath
Verdict: Howlingly advanced buggy
Price Guide
A £2500　　**B** £1300　　**C** £700
Current Maker: GT Mouldings, Brighton, Sussex

Dean Jeffries was a buggy god in America (and creator of the Pink Panther car) and it was his Kyote II that Steve Remp and Phil Ayres of Design Dynamics built in the UK. Over the unshortened VW chassis went possibly the prettiest and most modern-looking shape of the buggy era: an enveloping GRP body of exceptional strength, which unusually incorporated doors and an optional two-stage hardtop to turn it into a pick-up or an estate. Bodyshells were on the expensive side, so production was always limited. Moulds went to GP in 1976 and then, after about 15 years dormant, were revived by GT Mouldings.

Latham Super Sports

☆☆☆☆

Prod Years: 1983-90
Prod Numbers: 26
For: Performance potential, spacious interior, large boot, it's rare and does have its own following
Against: Dodgy panel fit, ugly humpy styling, too large for a sports car
Verdict: Wasted promise
Price Guide
A £3500　　**B** £1700　　**C** £700
Current Maker: None

What a long and drawn-out development period Paul and Julia Latham-Jackson's project had! The first prototype appeared at the Stoneleigh show in 1983, as a one-off XKSS lookalike on Triumph TR4 parts. From the Cornish base, a restyled production version was developed for mainly Dolomite parts; this did not arrive until the latter half of 1985, and even then it was not production-ready. A complicated central glassfibre monocoque was supplemented by front and rear steel subframes, steel-reinforced sills and honeycomb floor and bulkheads. Triumph rear axle, Triumph 1850, TR7 or Sprint engines, MGB windscreen.

Lemazone Comet

☆☆

Prod Years: 1984-87
Prod Numbers: Very few
For: Seating for four (just about), styling is not objectionable, simple VW Beetle basis
Against: No real improvement on the SN1 - itself a '70s has-been
Verdict: There are far better coupes around, even VW based ones
Price Guide
A £1400　　**B** £1000　　**C** £500
Current Maker: None

Lemazone was one of those bargain basement purveyors of plastic who managed to eke a living during the 1980s. They took on the Pulsar (see page 85) and SN1 (page 96) from Amplas, and also revived the Beaujangle (page 16). Their only attempt to move the breed on was the Comet, a revised version of the SN1. Its previously sharp-edged styling was given more rounded contours, but in all other respects it remained much the same as before: VW Beetle floorpan, 2+2 seating and a general hotch-potch of other parts to make a completed car. It's doubtful if this car even entered production.

Lenham Healey

☆☆☆☆☆

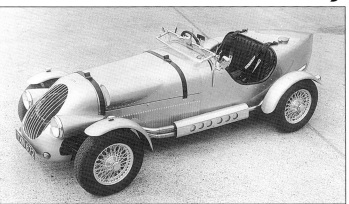

Prod Years: 1977-82
Prod Numbers: 20
For: Blistering performance thanks to light weight, nicely made, great character, rare
Against: Desperately stark, rather ugly, possibly worth more these days if you convert it back to a big Healey
Verdict: A real sports car in the true sense of the phrase
Price Guide
A £12,500　　**B** £8000　　**C** £4000
Current Maker: None

Lenham was a famous glassfibre panel maker which turned its attention, in 1977, to making a stark sports car out of an Austin-Healey. In style it echoed the great Healey Silverstone of 1949-51. The idea was to bring in your rusty old 'big' Healey and have it converted by the Kent factory (this was in the days when Healeys were not as collectable as they are now). The Lenham was an undoubted brute: it was 5cwt lighter than the Austin-Healey, thanks to its GRP bodywork and aluminium bonnet, and many took to the track. Some nice details like external handbrake, full instrumentation and tonneau cover.

Lightning GT

Real Corvettes could be bought pretty cheaply in the early 1980s, so why anyone would be interested in a sub-standard kit-form lookalike is a mystery. It didn't even really look much like a 'Vette. The Lightning was a glassfibre targa-topped two-seater based on a simple chassis designed to accept Cortina MkIII/IV mechanicals (including suspension and steering). Any Ford engine up to V6 could be fitted. You got winding windows but suffered with an acrylic plastic rear screen. It took the Stafford manufacturer over a year to get the car production-ready, but it then quickly disappeared from the scene.

Prod Years: 1984-85
Prod Numbers: Very few
For: Simplicity of Cortina donor bits, targa roof
Against: Offensive styling, poor quality, utterly un-exotic character, many details left unfinished
Verdict: Embarrassing
Price Guide
A £1200   **B** £700   **C** £300
Current Maker: None

Limited Edition Californian

Proof that beach buggies never die was provided by Limited Edition Sportscars of Warrington, Cheshire, when they produced an all-new one - in 1983. Their main trade was supplying accessories and as agents for other people's kits. The Californian Dune Buggy was a GP-style buggy with full-length side panels and a reasonable degree of sophistication. You could either source your own unmodified VW Beetle floorpan or opt for a specially-prepared chassis from Limited Edition. Predictably, the demand for buggies was pretty pale and the Californian proved to be a real Limited Edition.

Prod Years: 1983-84
Prod Numbers: Not many
For: A little more sophisticated than the average buggy, at least it won't have had as much time to deteriorate, fun rarely comes this cheap
Against: Mould quality no more than acceptable, oft-quoted buggy complaints of wet head, sore back and frozen elbow
Verdict: Send it back to California; they'll have more fun with it
Price Guide
A £1500   **B** £1000   **C** £500
Current Maker: None

Lomax 224

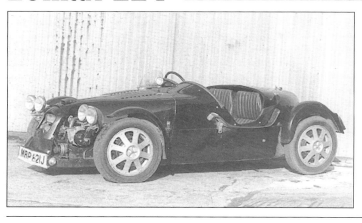

Glassfibre specialist Nigel Whall decided to use some spare capacity to design a GRP sports car, and came up with the 2CV-based Lomax. It was brilliantly simple: atop an unmodified Citroen A-Series floorpan (2CV/Dyane/Ami) sat a very simple double-scuttle body with some plywood and steel tube hoops. Thus it was very easy to build. It was called 224 because it had two cylinders, two seats and four wheels. The engine sat near-exposed at the front. Various body options followed: Continental bonnet covering more of the engine, flowing wings, doors and rear seats. Lomax also made a replacement 2CV 'pan and its own chassis.

Prod Years: 1983-date
Prod Numbers: Approx 500
For: No pretences, simple mechanicals, high economy, low prices, off-the-scale fun factor
Against: Pretty basic, weedy glassfibre, doesn't look as appealing as the trike version
Verdict: No-frills fun car
Price Guide
A £2700   **B** £1600   **C** £700
Current Maker: Lomax Motor Co, Halesowen, West Midlands

Lomax 223

Whall's prototype three-wheeler was in fact a four-wheeler, which he achieved by chopping off the rear chassis members and inverting the 2CV's trailing arms. But making a genuine trike was an obvious move, so Brian Mumford developed a modification of one of the rear arms with a 6in tube welded into it to make the rear wheel sit centrally. One of the inter-connected springs therefore had to be 'tied' at the back. Options included a proper windscreen and full hood, wire wheels and chromed parts. Lomax claimed (possibly correctly) that the 223 was the best-selling kit car in Britain during the late 1980s.

Prod Years: 1983-date
Prod Numbers: Approx 1800
For: Eccentric but lovable character, ingenious use of 2CV parts, cheap tax, huge fun
Against: Epic body roll, not as fast as it wants to be, mouldings rather thin
Verdict: Smile-inducing
Price Guide
A £3000   **B** £2200   **C** £1000
Current Maker: Lomax Motor Co, Halesowen, West Midlands

Lomax 424/423

☆☆☆

Prod Years: 1985-date
Prod Numbers: Quite a few
For: Indecently fast, surprisingly good around corners, similar mechanical simplicity
Against: Front end looks pretty ugly (and the rest of it too, actually), same faults as 224
Verdict: Gloriously eccentric GTI frightener
Price Guide
A £3000   **B** £2000   **C** £1200
Current Maker: Lomax Motor Co, Halesowen, West Midlands

In 1972 Citroen launched a real Q-car in the form of the Ami Super - basically a 2CV-chassised saloon with the four-cylinder air-cooled engine from the GS. 1015cc may not sound much, but it developed 61bhp - possibly too much for the chassis to handle. You could use an Ami Super to make a Lomax 424 (two or three nutcases even made 423s, which were GS-powered trikes). 61bhp in a car weighing roughly 8cwt (450kg) made for an interesting time! Cornering was still pretty roly-poly but everyone who drove a 424 was amazed by its performance and handling. Easily identified by its rounded front end.

Lotus MkVI

☆☆☆☆☆☆

Prod Years: 1952-56
Prod Numbers: Approx 110
For: Ultra light weight, classic spindly style, easy to maintain, perfect for blatting round lanes and in historic racing
Against: Very rare and very expensive, it's the starkest thing on wheels
Verdict: An absolute classic Lotus, and first of the line
Price Guide
A £15,000   **B** £12,000   **C** £8000
Current Maker: None

Genius builder/racer Colin Chapman was persuaded to enter production with the MkVI after winning just about everything he entered. An ultra-basic sports machine, it had a space frame, aluminium body panels of the starkest nature, split Ford front beam axle, IFS and Ford live rear axle. Wide choice of engines, but mostly Ford Ten or MG TC. Always kit-built, quite comprehensive but totally unfinished. The pressures of Chapman's racing programme forced the MkVI out of production – much to the chagrin of amateur racers. Its excellent competition record makes it a great favourite of historic racers today.

Lotus XI

☆☆☆☆☆☆

Prod Years: 1956-60
Prod Numbers: 426
For: One of the best chassis ever seen, classic curvy bodywork, fantastic to drive and race, a joy all round
Against: Almost impossible to use as a road car these days, extremely expensive
Verdict: A1 collectable
Price Guide
A £38,000   **B** £30,000   **C** £25,000
Current Maker: None

While the XI (Eleven) was primarily a racing machine, it was conceived in the days when racers drove their cars to the event they would compete in. As such, the Eleven was offered complete with full lighting equipment and even a basic hood. Fabulous aerodynamic bodywork over a space frame. Three versions: Le Mans (Coventry-Climax power in 75, 83 or 100bhp forms, De Dion rear end), Club (75bhp Climax power and live axle/coil springs), and Sport (Ford sidevalve engine and live rear axle). Wishbone IFS after '56. Today, the XI makes an avidly sought-after historic racer.

Lotus Elite

☆☆☆☆☆☆

Prod Years: 1957-63
Prod Numbers: 998
For: Gloriously balanced handling, extremely handsome bodywork, historic in so many ways, pretty rapid with the right engine
Against: Costly, monocoque prone to cracking and very expensive to repair if crunched, noisy and hard-riding
Verdict: Justly viewed as a paragon
Price Guide
A £26,000   **B** £20,000   **C** £15,000
Current Maker: None

The incredible Elite proved that Colin Chapman was quite capable of producing fabulous road cars. It was a technical triumph: the world's first true production glassfibre monocoque (and exquisitely handsome too), IFS by wishbones and coils, Chapman struts at the rear, discs all round (inboard at the rear). Coventry-Climax alloy engines were light and powerful (up to 95bhp in the '62 Super 95 and more in the Super 100/105). SE of '60 had close-ratio ZF 'box. It lost Chapman's fledgling company a sackload of money but the Elite was hailed as a great car. Today, it's extremely collectable indeed.

Lotus Seven S1

★★★★★★

Chapman said he knocked the Seven off in a week; it has now lasted almost 40 years and become a British sports car institution. Space frame chassis, Lotus Eleven Club type rear suspension, modified Lotus Twelve front end, stressed aluminium body panels, Ford hydraulic drums. Power from Ford sidevalve, BMC A-series, or (as Super Seven) 75bhp 1098cc Coventry-Climax. Series 1 Seven is easily identified by its 'droopy' nose cone in aluminium and metal cycle wings up front. It may not be as fast or sophisticated as later Sevens but the S1 is every bit as much fun, and historically appealing too.

Prod Years: 1957-60
Prod Numbers: 242
For: Classic Chapman lightweight construction, simplicity, great handling, genuinely the best fun on a twisty lane, legendary aura surrounds it, S1 has a certain purity
Against: Some chassis flex, zero refinement, high prices, rare
Verdict: The original and ultimate bare-boned sports car
Price Guide
A £14,000   B £11,000   C £9500
Current Maker: None

Lotus Seven S2/S3

★★★★★★

The S2 Seven arrived in 1960, sporting flared GRP front and rear wings and a new GRP nose cone. The chassis was much simplified (fewer tubes), and the engine choices included Ford sidevalve or Anglia, BMC A-series and later (as the Super Seven) the 85bhp Cosworth 1340cc or 1498cc (up to 95bhp). Spitfire front discs from '62. The Seven almost died in 1966 when Lotus moved premises but demand persisted. Series 3 of 1968 got the Kent 1600 engine, Escort Mexico rear axle/drums, wider rear wings and uprated interior. Ultimate S3 Twin Cam had pukka Lotus power (13 built).

Prod Years: 1960-68/1968-70
Prod Numbers: 1350/350
For: Fabulous driver's car in all respects, superb fun on back lanes, a legend in Cosworth or Twin Cam form (worth more), an appreciating asset
Against: Stark, chassis more flexible than S1, expensive to buy
Verdict: Perhaps the best all-round Seven of them all
Price Guide
A £13,000   B £10,000   C £9000
Current Maker: None

Lotus Seven S4

★★★★★

With the S4, Lotus hoped to capture some of the Midget/Spitfire market and, to some extent, it succeeded, but it was not geared up to satisfying MG buyers' expectations on after-sales. The S4 was a total departure from earlier Sevens: an Alan Barrett styled all-glassfibre body bonded on to a new chassis, and an appearance which bordered on beach buggydom. Lotus Europa-type front suspension, Watts linkages at the rear. Cortina 1300/1600 and Lotus twin cam engine options. Soft and civilised when compared to other Sevens, but still fun. However, enthusiasts loathe the compromises and shun it.

Prod Years: 1970-73
Prod Numbers: Approx 900
For: More civilised than previous Sevens, still amazing abilities on the road, lots of fun, good value for a Lotus Seven
Against: Bonded structure is a nightmare to restore, poor image among Seven types, buggy-style interior
Verdict: Unloved, but that makes it a real bargain
Price Guide
A £9000   B £6000   C £4000
Current Maker: None

Lotus Elan S1

★★★★★★

Almost all Elans were sold as kits in Britain. One of the all-time greats of car design, and a benchmark handler, the Elan had a steel backbone chassis, a GRP body, independent suspension and all-round discs. Pop-up headlamps were a novelty for 1962 and overall dimensions were extremely compact. First cars had 1498cc engines, all subsequently uprated to the definitive 106bhp 1558cc twin cam unit. Expect 112mph and 0-60 in 8.5 secs. As the pure original iteration of the species, the S1 remains highly sought after, as the high prices reflect. A good one will reward you for years to come.

Prod Years: 1962-64
Prod Numbers: 900
For: Best-handling car of its day, superbly sweet engines, supremely chuckable, great performance, enthusiastic following
Against: Backbone chassis rusts, needs careful maintenance, high prices, S1s are rare
Verdict: The best kit car of all time?
Price Guide
A £15,000   B £12,000   C £7500
Current Maker: None

Marcos 3-Litre/2½-Litre/2-Litre

★★★★★

Prod Years: 1968-71/1971/1970-71
Prod Numbers: 350/11/40
For: Bigger engines provide impressive performance (120mph plus), nice interiors, strong following, good value
Against: Wooden chassis decay but then so do the metal ones
Verdict: The best of the classic Marcos models
Price Guide
A £10,000　**B** £7500　**C** £4500
Current Maker: None

More power was what the Marcos chassis had always called out for and it got it in 1968 when Jem Marsh fitted a Ford 3-litre V6 engine under the bonnet. Early 3-Litres had the old wooden chassis, but steel replaced it after about 100 cars. To please the US market, Marcos went to Volvo, fitting the 164 3-litre power unit in 1970. There was a short-lived 2½-Litre model in 1971 (Triumph TR6 engine), and a 2-Litre, fitted with a Ford V4 engine, which is worth 25% less than the figures quoted since it had far less performance – better to keep looking for a Ford V6 or Volvo engined car.

Marcos Mantis

★★★★★

Prod Years: 1970-71
Prod Numbers: 32
For: You can't get more individual, quite luxurious, full four seats, well-made, good performance
Against: You can't get away from that shape, weight is substantial
Verdict: Weird but only slightly wonderful, an acquired taste
Price Guide
A £6000　**B** £4000　**C** £2000
Current Maker: None

The Mantis has had a lot of bad publicity over the years: it has been slated over its 'rashers of bacon' styling and blamed for Marcos's crash of 1971. It's true that the shape did not come out quite as Dennis Adams had first intended, but it was not the main cause of Marcos's financial trouble. The first Marcos four-seater, it had a new semi-space frame chassis, lusty Triumph TR6 engine, GT6 IFS, coil-sprung live rear axle, and a luxurious interior. Surprisingly good ride and reasonable performance, but expensive in its day (even in kit form). Very rare, it has its own strong eccentrics-only following.

Marcos GT

★★★★★

Prod Years: 1981-91
Prod Numbers: Approx 220
For: The classic Marcos shape refined as the years progressed, V6 Martina Spyder is the pick of the bunch
Against: Archaic Triumph suspension on pre-'90 cars
Verdict: Still one of the great British sports cars
Price Guide
A £12,000　**B** £7500　**C** £4000
Current Maker: None

Jem Marsh continued to provide spares and support for Marcos cars after the 1971 liquidation and was persuaded to re-enter manufacture in 1981. This he did with a lightly reworked version of the old Dennis Adams two-seater. This time the chassis was a square tube space frame and the engines were exclusively Ford - one of any number of four-cylinder or V6 units. In 1991, the Cortina MkIV/V based Martina was launched to replace the old type: Mantula-style bodywork but non-V8 engines (fours, and Dagenham or Cologne V6) - see Volume 4 for full description. Marcos sold only fully-built cars from 1994 on.

Marcos Mantula

★★★★★

Prod Years: 1984-94
Prod Numbers: Approx 200
For: Amazing grunt and handling, butch character, easy to drive, well-built, comfortable interior
Against: Doesn't look as good as the original 'pure' shape
Verdict: The ultimate kit-built Marcos
Price Guide
A £17,500　**B** £10,500　**C** £6500
Current Maker: None

Jem Marsh and Dennis Adams had been working on a Rover V8 powered version of the GT as early as 1983, although it took a while longer to become available. It was what the chassis had been crying out for. Any Rover V8 engine/gearbox could be fitted, providing shattering levels of performance. Adams restyled the body to incorporate flared wings, small side skirts and a front spoiler, while underneath the new Marcos got a Sierra diff and Panhard rod. A very attractive Spyder was introduced in 1986 (see volume 4). There were optional styling kits and a big rear spoiler for the wild look.

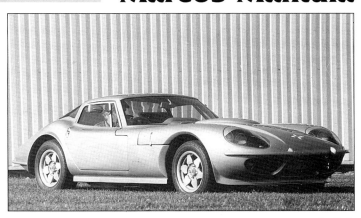

Mini-Marcos MkI/II/III

☆☆☆☆

The Mini-Marcos was born out of the DART prototype (as was the very similar Minijem). Of all-glassfibre monocoque construction, it used complete front and rear Mini sub-frames bolted through metal plates. Basic kits started at just £199, so it was no surprise that this was a rather crude machine. Biggest claim to fame was being the only British finisher at Le Mans in '66. Improved slightly until the Marcos firm's demise in 1971. Local West Country enthusiast Rob Walker then took it on and made it with a rear hatch and winding windows; from 1975-81 it was made by Harold Dermott's D&H Fibreglass Techniques of Oldham.

Prod Years: 1965-71
Prod Numbers: 1260 (all Mini-Marcos)
For: Light weight means high performance potential, well proven handling, it's cute in a way
Against: Pretty darned crude, cramped, not what you'd exactly call a beauty, old ones can get to look very shabby
Verdict: Amazingly successful ugly duckling
Price Guide
A £3000   **B** £1700   **C** £800
Current Maker: None

Mini-Marcos MkIV

☆☆☆☆

After Marcos went bust at the end of 1971, a small factory was purchased at Westbury and went into production with the new MkIV Mini-Marcos. This was four inches longer than before, allowing space for a small children's rear seat, while there were winding windows and a new opening tail-gate. Rob Walker made it briefly before the project was taken over and much improved by Harold Dermott's D&H Fibreglass Techniques in 1975. He made it until 1981, by which time his Midas had made the Mini-Marcos obsolete (though see Volume 4 for '91 MkV with new spoiler, wide arches etc).

Prod Years: 1971-81
Prod Numbers: see MkI/II/III
For: Extra seats in the rear, it's got a hatchback so you can now put your frozen peas in more easily, it looks a little a less ugly than earlier ones
Against: Still very crude by most standards, getting in the back is very nearly impossible
Verdict: Still a fun package, still an ugly bugger
Price Guide
A £3000   **B** £1700   **C** £800
Current Maker: None

Marlin Roadster

☆☆☆☆☆☆

From his base in Plymouth, Paul Moorhouse produced one of the most successful and best engineered of all kits. Neatly styled, it combined aluminium and glassfibre body panels over a tubular chassis intended initially for Triumph Herald/Vitesse/Spitfire mechanicals. In 1981, a Marina live axle was adopted, as a prelude to the Marina becoming the standard donor vehicle, and doors were then standardised. Alfa, Fiat, Ford and Rover V8 engines were also commonly fitted. Marlin sold the Roadster to Yorkshire's YKC Engineering in 1992, keeping its own recently-launched new car, the Cabrio (see volume 4).

Prod Years: 1979-date
Prod Numbers: Approx 1500
For: Integrity of engineering, aluminium main body, very neat styling, compact dimensions and light weight, superb quality throughout, plenty to choose from
Against: Sorry - we don't feel like nitpicking
Verdict: Thoroughly together and desirable little roadster
Price Guide
A £5000   **B** £3000   **C** £1200
Current Maker: Yorkshire Kit Cars

Marlin Berlinetta

☆☆☆☆☆☆

Although it looks very much like the Roadster in profile, Marlin's Berlinetta was all-new and much larger, the intention being to produce a car which had 2+2 seating while at the same time being just as simple to build. Thus the single donor was the Ford Cortina, from which most components were taken (Sierra and Fiat engined versions followed). Familiar aluminium body and glassfibre wings/nose/scuttle/tail over a steel chassis, bottom-hinged boot with external spare, double-skinned ally doors with (gasp!) winding windows and optional removable hard top. Along with the Roadster, it migrated to YKC in 1992.

Prod Years: 1984-date
Prod Numbers: Approx 475
For: Just as pretty as the Roadster, really very practical, surprisingly civilised, very exacting standards of manufacture
Against: Not a lot apart from lack of driver's elbow room!
Verdict: Very convincing in every department
Price Guide
A £8000   **B** £5000   **C** £2000
Current Maker: Yorkshire Kit Cars, Elvington, York

Maya GT

☆☆☆

Prod Years: 1967-69
Prod Numbers: 6
For: Unusual Mini-based machine, simple mechanically and rust-free, 2+2 seating possible
Against: Silly-looking headlamps (the rest of the car looks a bit funny too)
Verdict: Odd left-over of the '60s Mini-based kit era
Price Guide
A £1200   **B** £750   **C** £400
Current Maker: None

A split between George Holmes, the creator of the Camber GT (see page 21), and his agent led to the axing of that model and its re-introduction as the Maya GT. The very last Camber had sported a new headlamp arrangement of cowled square headlamps. The Maya reverted to circular lamps, but positioned higher up with little eyebrows behind them, which meant that they were at least legal, unlike the too-low lamps of the early Cambers. Holmes' untimely death ended production prematurely. Amazingly the moulds for the Maya still exist. Values are likely to rise.

MC Acer

☆☆☆

Prod Years: 1984-date
Prod Numbers: 8
For: High quality, may have four seats, classic 'fifties look
Against: Dull looks, why not buy an original Turner?
Verdict: If you want a 1950s special with a Vauxhall Viva engine, this one is for you
Price Guide
A £1400   **B** £950   **C** £500
Current Maker: Ian Birks, Sheffield

The first of the 1960s nostalgia kit revivals, the MC Acer was basically a Turner re-engineered by Mark Clarkson for modern mechanicals. It was designed around either Vauxhall Viva or Ford Escort parts, although it quoted several other possible donors, including Hillman Avenger, Datsun 120Y, Morris Marina and Triumph Spitfire/Dolomite. In all cases, the propshaft and steering column needed to be shortened. On top of a cross-braced tubular steel chassis sat a pre-mounted and fairly thick GRP body, which had two or 2+2 seating. Imp tank, Mini headlamps and heater. Sheffield based MC Cars passed the Acer on to Carlton Mouldings.

MCA Coupe/Cabriolet

☆☆☆☆☆

Prod Years: 1983-96
Prod Numbers: A few
For: Very well made and well engineered, quite cute, attractive and surprisingly spacious interior, capable handling and roadholding
Against: Little Fiat engine needs mighty tuning to deliver anything like decent performance
Verdict: Treat it as a modern Fiat-Abarth special and it's not bad
Price Guide
A £2000   **B** £1200   **C** £500
Current Maker: None

This unassuming little sports car was a surprise to everyone who drove it. A not particularly inspiring-looking coupe with a 594cc Fiat 126 engine in the tail might not sound too promising, but Italian ex-racing driver Aurelio Bezzi's MCA was charming in its simplicity. The specification was simple: a steel tube chassis, separate GRP body panels, two seats and all Fiat 126 parts. After Bezzi emigrated, the little MCA passed to Minari briefly before going to Dash Sportscars, who offered a Cabriolet version too. In 1994, it went to IPS Developments, makers of the Hadleigh, but it lasted only a couple of years with them.

McCoy

☆☆☆

Prod Years: 1984-date
Prod Numbers: Approx 20
For: Corners very well, glassfibre quality impressive, 2+2 seating, decent boot, economical Mini basis
Against: Looks like a Clan on stilts
Verdict: Not really the real thing
Price Guide
A £2500   **B** £1500   **C** £700
Current Maker: McCoy Cars, Fakenham, Norfolk

If the McCoy looks like a Clan Crusader, that should come as no surprise, since the same man was responsible for styling both (ex-Lotus man John Frayling). Unlike the rear-engined Clan, the McCoy used a front-mounted Mini engine, complete with both its subframes, in a glassfibre monocoque body. This made the car much taller than the low-slung Clan, and consequently a bit silly-looking. There was even an estate version with a full four seats, bizarrely called the McIvoy. An alternative power source was the Metro. The McCoy has managed to last so long in production because the manufacturers rely on general GRP work.

Merlin TF

☆☆☆☆☆

The Merlin originated in the USA under the name Witton and had a VW Beetle engine in the tail (!). Although briefly offered here in that guise (one sold!), the definitive UK version was much modified by Essex-based Thoroughbred Cars: it had a separate chassis and all Cortina MkIII/IV/V parts (though special trailing arm and Panhard rod rear suspension). The Merlin's best feature was its rakish 1930s style, realised in glassfibre. 2+2 Monro (see below) from 1983, German TUV approval gained in 1986, Sierra-based chassis option from 1992. Lotus had some input on chassis design after early criticisms.

Prod Years: 1980-84
Prod Numbers: Approx 300
For: A shape which schoolboys would have dreamed about, good ol' Ford mechanical bits
Against: Early chassis was dubious, glassfibre moulding quality variable, hoods are basic
Verdict: Great-looking stalwart of the kit industry
Price Guide
A £5000   **B** £3000   **C** £1500
Current Maker: Merlin Sports Cars, Southend-on-Sea

Merlin Monro/Plus Two

☆☆☆☆☆

In 1983, Thoroughbred Cars came up with a 2+2 version of the Merlin, but why they called it the Monro is a mystery. In any case, it was quickly renamed the Plus Two and effectively replaced the TF. Both the chassis and rear suspension had to be redesigned and the rear bodywork was squared up to free as much space as possible, although there was really only ever enough room for two small children. They got a scooped-out floor, at least. Kit prices were roughly £300 more than the two-seater, and it proved a popular model. The parent company changed to Paris Cars in 1985, though Merlin continued as the trading name.

Prod Years: 1983-date
Prod Numbers: Approx 700
For: Same basic great shape but now two more passengers (or your luggage) can enjoy it, Ford parts make life easy
Against: Lacks the purity of line of the two-seater, early chassis and quality problems
Verdict: Now you can squeeze Marilyn in the back
Price Guide
A £6500   **B** £3700   **C** £1500
Current Maker: Merlin Sports Cars

Metaline

☆☆☆☆☆

One of the earliest British Cobra replicas was created by a Berkshire piano tuner, with the unique feature of an all-aluminium body. But this was very much a marginal product and it took several years for a true kit-form car to arrive. Semi-space frame powder-coated chassis, semi-monocoque one-piece body in GRP (later with Kevlar strengthening). Jaguar running gear with optional anti-roll bars, custom-made steering rack and pedals. Any small or big-block V8 engine was suitable, including very high output units. Metaline prices started low, but most customers spent large sums on coachbuilt replicas.

Prod Years: 1981-date
Prod Numbers: Approx 20
For: Much enhanced specification over the AC Cobra, high quality in evidence throughout, early aluminium body would be attractive
Against: Repair of damaged structure could be difficult, not many around
Verdict: Specialist product with appeal for the individualist
Price Guide
A £22,000 **B** £15,000 **C** £9000
Current Maker: Metaline, Wisbech, Cambs

MFE Magic

☆☆

Quite what was the 'magic' of which this machine's manufacturers were speaking is not recorded. This was, in fact, a fairly crude and odd-looking kit car aimed at the Dutton end of the market. The stylist (Roger Mossop of MG specialists, Motorspeed of Tangmere, West Sussex) created a weird fun/trad cross-over for MGB parts. The chassis was redesigned in 1985 to accept Cortina MkIII suspension and power train, though the Ford prop and exhaust needed shortening because the wheelbase was kept the same. Forward-hinging bonnet, gelcoat finish. Came to rest at Scorhill Motors, who went bust in 1996.

Prod Years: 1984-96
Prod Numbers: Approx 80
For: Originality, honesty, light weight, good quality glassfibre, high degree of chuckability
Against: Desperately basic hood, handling not properly sorted, styling is pretty weird
Verdict: A real kit car, and not a very enamouring second-hand prospect
Price Guide
A £1600   **B** £800   **C** £300
Current Maker: None

Midas/Midtec Bronze

☆☆☆☆☆

Prod Years: 1978-date
Prod Numbers: Approx 370
For: 100% rust free, lightweight, tough, legendary handling, fabulous point-to-point speed, economy, 2+2 seating, cheap to run, quality
Against: High scuttle line, cramped interior, getting a bit long-in-the-tooth, avoid crash-damaged cars
Verdict: Gordon Murray bought one - so should you
Price Guide
A £4500   B £2600   C £1200
Current Maker: Midtec, Leicester

Conceived by Harold Dermott (now production manager at McLaren) and designed by industry professional Richard Oakes, the Midas was one of the first of a new generation of kit cars for the 1980s. Unusual in having a chassis-less monocoque body made entirely of glassfibre. Complete Mini front subframe, steel rear beam, any A-series engine. Kits were mostly very up-market compared to the standards of the day. Later ones had revised bumpers including foglamps. Overshadowed in later years by the Metro-based Midas Gold, and a victim of Midas' collapse in 1989. Briefly made by Pastiche Cars, then revived by Midtec Sports Cars in 1992.

Milano

☆☆☆

Prod Years: 1984-86
Prod Numbers: Approx 40
For: Uses many Alfa parts, great (very Alfa-like) to drive, high quality hood, a four-seat convertible (and that's rare), pretty shape
Against: Quality not always very good, long since out of production
Verdict: Flawed but enticing
Price Guide
A £4000   B £2500   C £1000
Current Maker: None

One thing that old Alfa Romeos do well is rust, leaving gorgeous engines and 'boxes left in an orange puddle. Simon Hilton's solution to this problem was the Milano. He took everything out of a GTV and put it in his own multi-tube steel chassis - and that included the front bulkhead, windscreen, dashboard and doors. The bodywork was naturally glassfibre and was inspired by Pininfarina's XJS prototype. All interior trim, seats and carpets also came from the Alfa GTV. Not the easiest kit to build. S&J Motor Engineers also built a second model called the Sportiva, but that remained a prototype.

Minijem

☆☆☆

Prod Years: 1966-76
Prod Numbers: Approx 350
For: Prettier than a Mini-Marcos, light weight means good performance, low centre of gravity means tight handling, bit of a cutey
Against: Always rather crudely built, cramped inside
Verdict: Little GT jem for Mini fans
Price Guide
A £2250   B £1250   C £700
Current Maker: None

Test pilot Dizzy Addicot's DART prototype sired not only the Mini-Marcos, but also the Minijem, named after Jeremy Delmar-Morgan. Unlike the aluminium prototype, the body was a glassfibre monocoque with wood and steel reinforcement. Mini mechanicals. Rob Statham took over production in 1967 and released a reshaped MkII version in 1969. His firm went bust in 1971 and the Jem was revived by Wiltshire (later Yorkshire) based High Performance Mouldings, who added a tailgate. Finally arrived chez Malcolm Fell who developed a MkIII model for launch in 1975. The later Kingfisher Sprint was based on a Minijem.

Minus

☆☆☆

Prod Years: 1982-date
Prod Numbers: Approx 220
For: Chopped Mini looks, no rusty shell to worry about, all ancillaries derive from the Mini so are easy to replace, light weight
Against: Cramped inside, check Mini rear subframe for rust
Verdict: Look mum, someone's sat on me Mini
Price Guide
A £3500   B £1900   C £700
Current Maker: Minus Cars, New Buckenham, Norfolk

Brian Luff, creator of all the Status kits listed separately, was the design talent behind the Minus (indeed it was initially launched as the Status Mini Minus). He created a modern GRP reinterpretation of the chopped 1960s Minisprint. Deseamed style, body-shell strengthened with a bonded-in steel roll-over hoop and extra steel around the door frames. All Mini interior trim, glass, lights and opening panels, plus shortened Mini doors. The kit was productionised by Keith Lain's Minus Cars. The whole Minus project came up for sale in 1994 but is still offered by Minus Cars at the time of writing.

Mongoose

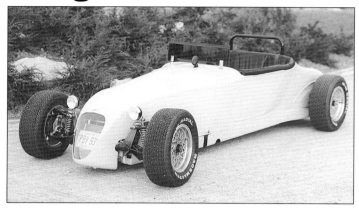

Although it's a borderline hot rod (and we don't cover those in this guide), the Mongoose is worth a listing because so many were made and so many famous companies took it on. It was developed by Terry Sands' Muscle City as a vague 1927 Model T racer kit, which distinguished itself by having independent suspension all round. Cortina MkIII mechanicals. Sands' company became Sandwood Automotive, then taken over by Sheldonhurst, which went bust in a fairly short space of time. DJ's early association with Terry Sands led them to offer the Mongoose but they never really pushed it and it simply faded away.

Prod Years: 1980-86
Prod Numbers: Quite a few
For: Silly appearance, very light weight, immense performance potential, attention creator
Against: Silly appearance, no weather protection, standard of finish totally dependent on builder
Verdict: The only street rod with street cred
Price Guide
A £4000 **B** £1800 **C** £400
Current Maker: None

Mosquito

Not much is known about the Mini-based Mosquito trike since it was never advertised or featured in any of the usual magazines like *Hot Car* and *Custom Car*. However, there are several survivors of a short production run of five cars. It was conceived by a company based in Hereford in about 1976 and had a curious little open-topped glassfibre body atop Mini mechanicals with a single rear wheel. Some had a GRP roll-over bar and solid sidescreens. In modified form it was revived as the Triad in the early 1990's by new company, Malvern Autocraft of Malvern, Worcs (see Volume 4).

Prod Years: 1976-77
Prod Numbers: 5
For: Space pod styling (with neat side-mounted exhausts), all Mini bits, pretty practical, cheap to run, good fun on a sunny day
Against: Too bizarre for some tastes, skips and jumps around on bumpy roads, horrible in the rain
Verdict: Intriguing also-ran
Price Guide
A £1700 **B** £1000 **C** £500
Current Maker: None

Moss Roadster

Specials expert John Cowperthwaite scored great success with this kit, the first to cash in on a latent demand for cheaper Morgan-style cars. Based on a lightly modified Herald/Vitesse chassis, it was cheap, pretty and easy to build. The 2+2 Malvern version arrived in 1983. There was later a Moss Triumph replacement chassis or an all-new chassis for Ford engines (from late 1983). Production faltered around a factory fire in 1985 and everything came to rest with Hampshire Classics, and thence to three Moss club members in Bath. A brand new chassis arrived in 1992, also able to take Rover V8 engines and Sierra parts.

Prod Years: 1981-date
Prod Numbers: Approx 500
For: Nice shape, cheap to run, plenty around to choose from at good, affordable prices
Against: Quality variable, never very sophisticated in engineering terms
Verdict: Much-loved stalwart of the kit car business
Price Guide
A £4500 **B** £2300 **C** £1000
Current Maker: Moss Cars, Rush Hill, Bath

Moss Malvern

Increasing practicality was a trait which most kit car companies embraced in the 1980s and Moss led the early wave with its 1983 Malvern, a 2+2 version of the established Roadster. The Malvern name strongly hinted at the inspirations, if not the execution. The Herald/Vitesse mechanical side remained identical but the bodywork was revised to find enough room for two children in the back, and the weather gear was extended in a tent-like fashion to give them protection. Later options of Moss's own chassis for Triumph or Ford parts also applied here. There's still a strong following for these cars.

Prod Years: 1983-date
Prod Numbers: Approx 500
For: All the virtues of the Roadster with the added bonus of seating for four in fair comfort
Against: Not quite as handsome as the two-seater (2+2s never are), some early quality problems
Verdict: Very familiar old face
Price Guide
A £4500 **B** £2300 **C** £1000
Current Maker: Moss Cars, Rush Hill, Bath

O&C Sprint

☆☆☆☆

Prod Years: 1984-88
Prod Numbers: A few
For: Well-engineered chassis and good suspension meant excellent handling and roadholding.
Against: Lousy aerodynamics blunt performance, not very pretty
Verdict: Basic, no-frills sports car which couldn't decide if it was a Caterham or a Morgan
Price Guide
A £2200   **B** £1500   **C** £750
Current Maker: None

The Sprint had a more traditionally styled body than the Sport, but it was a strange hotch-potch of styles: you got 1930s style flowing front and rear wings, little doors, a full windscreen and weather gear, but there was an odd split grille and a massive 'spoiler' which looked more like an iron girder stuck out at the front. Basis was Marina/Minor/Escort/Toyota. It was unusual in that its bodywork was an all-steel mono-coque. You could choose whether you wanted doors or not, and there was a choice of flowing or cycle front wings. Kits were very cheap at £675 plus tax.

O&C Sonnet

☆☆☆☆

Prod Years: 1985-88
Prod Numbers: Very few
For: A good handler, light weight, more practical than many Seven-type kits, high-level fun factor
Against: Awkwardly styled, difficult to get into (no doors), Minor/Marina 1.3 engines aren't something you'd let slip in pub parleys
Verdict: Semi-practical sports/race cross-over
Price Guide
A £2000   **B** £1400   **C** £750
Current Maker: None

The Sonnet was similar in construction to the Sport, sharing the idea of its pressed steel body/chassis and roll-over frame, but it was less of an out-and-out racer for the road, and more of a practical dual purpose machine. As such it had more stylised front and rear sections in glassfibre, enveloping front wings, a lockable boot and a fixed windscreen. You could base it on either Marina 1.3 or Minor parts, and kit prices started from a very cheap £599 plus tax, and an extra £147 for the competition pack. O&C also offered a swoopy sports car called the Serac but probably none of these was built.

O&C Thruxton

☆☆☆☆

Prod Years: 1985-88
Prod Numbers: Very few
For: Wide adaptability, proven ability on the track, light weight
Against: Crude manufacture, ugly as hell, difficult to finish
Verdict: Made some impression on the track, but that was more than 10 years ago
Price Guide
A £2000   **B** £1400   **C** £750
Current Maker: None

Oldham & Crowther's Thruxton was more competition orientated than the Sport and Sonnet, but was nevertheless a dual purpose car. O&C described this as "for the advanced builder", and you can see why. It had no specific donor, being designed to accept virtually any engine up to a Rover V8, thanks to a simple chassis design. Pressed steel main body/chassis unit as per normal O&C practice was designed to accept a variety of coil/spring and wishbone suspensions systems, plus a live rear axle with Panhard rod (or optional IRS). The front wings were made of GRP, as were the solid cockpit cover and dashboard.

Opus HRF

 ☆☆

Prod Years: 1966-72
Prod Numbers: Approx 220
For: Wild bucket style, preposterously rapid, vintage feel, interesting around corners...
Against: ...a bit too interesting for most of us, quality pretty dire, miserable in the wet
Verdict: The old Opus Pocus has well and truly faded by now
Price Guide
A £1200   **B** £600   **C** £200
Current Maker: None

Better not be too rude about this one, since the publisher of this book owns one. Nevertheless, for objectivity's sake, it was a strange old crate: Neville Trickett designed it according to the bath tub school of styling, it was dead cheap at £99 for the body/chassis kit, and earned a reputation for precarious road manners. It was tiny, weighed just 8cwt (400kg) and could go indecently fast. Suspension was a mix of Ford Pop and Anglia, the front wheels were Mini and the recommended engine was Cortina 1600. HRF stood for Hot Rod Ford, by the way. Original purveyors passed it on to Lambert in 1970.

Panache

If ever there was a misnomer for a car, this was it. The Panache had absolutely none of the aforementioned stuff. It was basically an early attempt by Paul Lawrenson at a Countach 'lookalike', initially for a full length VW Beetle floorpan. The body incorporated a Bond Bug-style flop-forward canopy. The Panache was brought to production by Bob Davies' Panache Kit Cars of Darwen, Lancs, who laughably described it as "the most exotic and futuristic component car available". A special chassis was developed for mid-mounted engines up to V8s, but was as dire as the rest of the car. Also briefly made a more accurate LP400 replica.

Prod Years: 1983-87
Prod Numbers: Approx 70
For: Styling is at least distinctive (ahem)
Against: Awful quality, difficult to build (so many left unfinished), both VW and mid-engined versions stank, no merits whatsoever
Verdict: Panache? You have got to be joking
Price Guide
A £3000   **B** £2000   **C** £700
Current Maker: None

Parabug

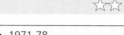

If by some strange quirk of fate you are a fanatic of both cubism and military vehicles, then the Parabug must be your ideal car. Made by North East Fibreglass of Aberdeen, a boat builder by trade, it was a jeep-style thing intended for a VW Beetle floorpan. GRP quality was good and you got things like rolled return edges, stressed bodywork and a fold-flat windscreen which fixed by magnets. Colour choices were Jungle Green, Panzer Grey, Desert Yellow, Marine Blue and Scorched Earth! Optional nerf bars, special seats (which weren't very good) and weather gear (equally poor). They don't make 'em like they used to.

Prod Years: 1971-78
Prod Numbers: A few
For: Novel appearance, rigid body, good ground clearance at the front
Against: Crap ground clearance at the back, poor hood, dodgy detailing, zero refinement, people will think you're a born-again Nazi
Verdict: Jeep at the price
Price Guide
A £1000   **B** £600   **C** £200
Current Maker: None

Pelland Sports

Peter Pellandine co-made the Ashley and Falcon in the 1960s before emigrating to Australia. There he made the Pelland Sports from 1974. He returned to Britain in 1978 and launched the Sports in 1979. It was a GRP monocoque with a tubular steel cockpit cage and a rear subframe to accept a centrally-mounted Beetle or Ford engine, plus special rear suspension; the front end was standard Beetle. Right-mounted gear lever, just 9cwt, only 35in high with its optional targa/gullwing top in place. Project sold in 1980 to become the Ryder Rembrandt, and in 1982 to Graham Autos. Listair then modified it to make the Dash (qv).

Prod Years: 1979-86 (in UK)
Prod Numbers: Quite a few
For: Rakish lines, fine handling balance, lots of fun, no rust
Against: Highly impractical, check the windscreen is glass not perspex, no luggage space
Verdict: Strange but engaging buggy/Lotus 7 cross-over
Price Guide
A £1600   **B** £1000   **C** £500
Current Maker: None

Phoenix

An amazing collection of ex-Lotus people was involved with the Clan Crusader (see page 25). One of the main movers was Paul Haussauer (pronounced 'osserway'), whose trade continued to be general glassfibre work into the 1980s. His Phoenix was an ultra-worthy attempt to make a completely rust-free and practical car in kit form. It used untouched Mini subframes, reskinned doors and interior parts in a painted GRP monocoque body which was deliberately reminiscent of a Mini Clubman estate. It was expensive but easy to build and more practical than a Mini thanks to a bigger interior and proper tailgate.

Prod Years: 1983-86
Prod Numbers: Quite a few
For: Outstandingly economical, rust-free shell, good quality glassfibre, all Mini parts, good luggage capacity
Against: Devastatingly ordinary, rather boring to drive
Verdict: Deadly dull but will probably outlive its owner
Price Guide
A £1500   **B** £1000   **C** £500
Current Maker: None

Piper GT/GTT

☆☆☆☆☆

Prod Years: 1967-71
Prod Numbers: Approx 70
For: Sleek styling, high performance, race car bred handling
Against: Cramped interior, some restoration headaches, highly impractical, poor driver vision
Verdict: A strong following now exists for these unique British sports cars
Price Guide
A £7500 **B** £5000 **C** £2500
Current Maker: None

Produced by George Henrotte, a well-known Formula 3 manufacturer and engine preparer, the Piper was conceived as a way of recycling Austin Healey Sprite parts, though the production GTT was mostly Ford based. Tubular steel backbone chassis, Herald front end, Ford Corsair rear, usually Ford 1600 engine (some have Midget, Alfa, BDA or Twin Cam). Very low and sleek body was in GRP. After the first six cars, Brain Sherwood developed the GTT but he was killed in 1969. The company was continued by Bill Atkinson and Tony Waller. The 1969 show car had gullwing doors. Sold only in complete component form.

Piper P2

☆☆☆☆

Prod Years: 1971-74
Prod Numbers: Approx 40
For: More room inside than the GTT, prettier too, still the same intoxicating drive and unmistakable looks
Against: Still no opening windows and not really useable as an everyday car, poor driver vision
Verdict: Lithe beauty
Price Guide
A £7500 **B** £5000 **C** £2500
Current Maker: None

The Piper GTT was redesigned by the new faces at the factory in 1971 to become the P2. The chassis was a full six inches longer than the GTT's, giving it much better legroom. The rear axle became Capri, the arches were flared and the nose was significantly restyled to incorporate pop-up headlamps although they later reverted to fixed units. Overall, the car looked even more attractive and went better too. Financial problems sunk Berkshire based Piper Cars in 1971 but it was kick-started, moved to Lincolnshire and renamed Embrook Engineering; it didn't last long. Most P2s were sold fully-built.

Pilgrim Bulldog

☆☆☆

Prod Years: 1985-date
Prod Numbers: Approx 2200
For: Reasonable quality, used ones can be great value, massive following
Against: Marina based version not a great handler and looked funny, scuttle shake on early cars a problem
Verdict: Amazingly successful
Price Guide
A £5000 **B** £3000 **C** £1000
Current Maker: Pilgrim Cars, Henfield, Sussex

From very humble origins, Den Tanner and Bill Harling's Bulldog became a best-seller. It wasn't particularly pretty, its Marina basis wasn't exotic, but its price - just £650 for the body/chassis kit - was sensational, and it knocked Dutton off its pedestal. Simple ladder frame chassis, 2+2 seating. Radiator grille was an odd 'dragonfly's eyes' shape, replaced by a prettier front end from MkII of late 1985. Later changes included small doors from 1986, bigger doors on 1987 MkIII, Cortina donor for MkIV of late 1987. Revised in 1992 (MkV). Plenty of options available to make a good-looking car. About 40 MkI Bulldogs made.

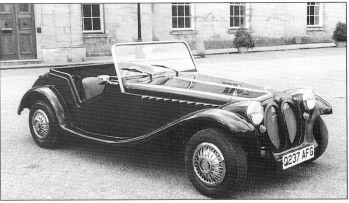

Powerbug

☆☆

Prod Years: 1970-71
Prod Numbers: Approx 150
For: All the fun of the buggy fayre
Against: And all of its misery too, plus the lights are illegal
Verdict: Just another buggy
Price Guide
A £1300 **B** £1000 **C** £500
Current Maker: None

A Bromley-based company called Powerspeed, run by the Aldridge family, produced the Powerbug by modifying the nose of a GP Buggy shell. It was in all respects an entirely conventional buggy which struggled to find its own identity. Its Vulture-style faired-in rectangular headlamps were so close-set that side lights had to be fitted to the wings to keep within the law. There were glassfibre shells to fit standard and shortened VW Beetle floorpans, priced at £153 and £143 respectively. Powerspeed would even fit Porsche, Corvair and V8 engines for you!

Probe 2001

Dennis Adams' amazing Probe series began as early as 1968 with the 29in high Probe 15, which never made production. Neither did the follow-up Probe 16 (three made). The true production Probe was the 2001. Still very low (37in high), it retained the mid-mounted BMC 1800 engine but had a redesigned body, now featuring a rear aerofoil for roll-over protection and an electrically-operated sliding perspex roof, through which you entered the car (the seats moved up and back to ease ingress). Adams built just four examples before the project moved to Scotland, to two different concerns, where around 12 further shells were made.

Prod Years: 1970-72
Prod Numbers: 16
For: Absolutely unique appearance, moving roof and seats are a great party trick, *Clockwork Orange* cool
Against: Dashed impractical, claustrophobic, iffy handling, getting the body repaired would be difficult
Verdict: The only way to out-FAB the Thunderbirds
Price Guide
A £3000   B £1600   C £900
Current Maker: None

Pulsar 2

The Concept Centaur Mk2 had just been launched when it passed to Mirage Developments of Biggin Hill to become the Pulsar 2. The Mk2 was taller and more practical than the Mk1 Centaur, and featured 2+2 seating, conventional doors, a rear three-quarter light and a Vauxhall Ventora curved windscreen. Without the rear seats and window behind the cockpit, the car was called the Pulsar 3 (see below). The Imp engine and running gear were retained, although Ford and Mini engine conversion kits were offered. Passed in 1980 to MR Developments of Trowbridge but it didn't last long.

Prod Years: 1978-82
Prod Numbers: Approx 30 (all types)
For: Well made, wild looks, does actually drive pretty well, soundly engineered
Against: So far diluted from the original Probe that it looks very odd, claustrophobic, underpowered in Imp guise, poor visibility
Verdict: Strange fish
Price Guide
A £1200   B £800   C £600
Current Maker: None

Pulsar 3

The wierdly styled 2+2 Pulsar 2 was a semi-practical device, but it had lost much of the Probe's dramatic looks. The Pulsar 3 set out to remedy that. While it retained the Pulsar 2's front end styling and conventional doors, it did away with the rather odd raised rear roof and glass section in favour of a sloping tail and one-piece opening hatchback. That meant it could only be a strict two-seater. The tiny rear three-quarter windows were modified too. Usually Imp basis, but optional Ford and Mini based kits were advertised in the specialist press late in the day.

Prod Years: 1978-82
Prod Numbers: See Pulsar 2
For: Nothing else looks remotely like it (and it's more successful than the Pulsar 2), well conceived, very rare
Against: Highly impractical, Imp engine not really powerful enough, gawky from some angles, not for claustrophobics
Verdict: An extreme rarity
Price Guide
A £1200   B £800   C £600
Current Maker: None

Pulsar

This was a not-very-convincing Porsche 911 style car with a full convertible roof and VW components. However, you didn't have to use a chopped-down Beetle pan: instead you were supplied with a box section steel chassis with subframes front and rear, pre-drilled to take a VW front axle, steering, pedals, special rear suspension and any VW or Porsche engine. The self-coloured GRP body boasted wind-up windows, Citroen GS screen, integral floor and moulded dash. Optional Carrera/Turbo bodykits, soft top and roll bar. Launched by Amplas of Chalgrove, Oxon, but soon assumed by Lancashire-based Lemazone.

Prod Years: 1984-87
Prod Numbers: Quite a few
For: Cheap prices, I suppose it looks a bit like a Porsche, you can use the rear spoiler as a picnic table
Against: Beetle engine, sore pastiche of 911 style, chassis is rugged rather than clever, lack of quality plainly in abundance
Verdict: More of a Porker than a Porsche
Price Guide
A £2750   B £1700   C £1100
Current Maker: None

Puma

☆☆☆☆☆

Prod Years: 1966-84
Prod Numbers: Approx 30,000
For: Extremely attractive styling (Bertone was a fan), simple VW basis, high quality glassfibre work
Against: You'll have a tough job finding one in the UK, getting parts may prove difficult
Verdict: Worth pouncing on
Price Guide
A £5000   **B** £2500   **C** £1000
Current Maker: None

We haven't included many imported kits in this guide, but the Brazilian-made Puma was exceptional. It first appeared as the DKW-Malzoni in 1964 and progressed to Volkswagen Beetle basis in 1966 to become the Puma. Very elegant coupe and convertible styles were offered with various type designations: GT, GTE, GTS and GTC. Imported to the UK by The Chequered Flag in 1973 before Ford objected to the use of the name here. As a result very few were actually imported, although many European countries received quite a number of Pumas. One of the most successful specialist cars ever, as production figures confirm.

Python

☆☆☆☆☆☆

Prod Years: 1981-93
Prod Numbers: 97
For: Tremendously strong and competent chassis, very high quality all round, suits taller drivers
Against: Won't satisfy sticklers for authenticity, rather heavy
Verdict: Top Cobra replica under the skin, well worth searching out
Price Guide
A £22,000   **B** £17,000   **C** £9000
Current Maker: None

Unique Autocraft always took a rather laid-back approach to the business of making kit cars. Born out of Pete & Mart's Rod & Custom, UA took a different tack to Cobra replication: their chassis was not a Cobra clone but an over-engineered box section steel chassis which quickly gained a reputation as the toughest around. It also allowed the cockpit to be two inches longer than standard. Suspension was independent by Jaguar XJ, steering by Triumph Dolomite, engines from Ford V6 to big block V8. Left production in 1993 but all the jigs and moulds still exist and it may re-enter production soon.

Radbourne Abarth

☆☆☆☆☆

Prod Years: 1968-71
Prod Numbers: 12
For: Beautiful shape, genuine Abarth credentials, fine handling, Mini Cooper-crushing performance, great curiosity value
Against: Survival rate, high prices if you ever do find one
Verdict: It's basically a real Abarth, with everything that brings
Price Guide
Probably between £10,000 and £20,000
Current Maker: None

What's this? A kit-form Abarth? This curious tale of a British-made Abarth begins with London-based Radbourne's director on holiday in Turin, where he located 30 unsold aluminium Abarth-Simca bodyshells, which he bought and returned to England. There he sold complete, fully-trimmed kits at a fairly hefty £1350, with Simca 1000 chassis platforms and modified Abarth suspension, plus Fiat 124 engines bored out to 1280cc. However, of the 30 bodyshells, only 12 were in good enough condition to be sold; the remainder were used for spares.

Ram SC/SEC

☆☆☆☆☆

Prod Years: 1984-date
Prod Numbers: Approx 830
For: Race-proven Reynard chassis, visually a high degree of authenticity, quality workmanship, 4x4 version is a talking point, successful on the track
Against: Expensive
Verdict: Carroll Shelby can't be all wrong – this is one of the best
Price Guide
A £25,000   **B** £18,000   **C** £7500
Current Maker: Ram Automotive, Maldon, Essex

Adrian Cocking, ex of DJ Sportscars, set up on his own to make sports replicas from 1984. The company was called LR Roadsters and all cars were called Ram. The first was a Cobra replica, whose main distinguishing feature was a round-tube backbone space frame chassis designed by Adrian Reynard. Suspension was Jaguar, naturally, while steering was MGB, pedals were Marina and engines were usually small block V8. Glassfibre body or, from 1991, a choice of aluminium. Interesting four-wheel drive Cosworth version launched in 1993 while the SEC is Ford-based. Carroll Shelby's 1994 grant of official approval for the Ram was a real coup.

Ram LM/SS

☆☆☆☆☆☆

Ram's other early replica was the D-Type (which like the Cobra was called by a moniker - LM, denoting Le Mans). It shared the Reynard chassis developed for the Cobra replica, with the distinction that it could be fitted with any of the Jaguar range of straight six engines, which were much more in keeping than Yankee V8s. Glassfibre bodywork in a variety of styles: long and short nose, fixed and detachable rear fins, and an XKSS bodystyle (dubbed the SS). In all forms, the replication was impeccable and much effort was invested to get the right replica parts, including interiors.

Prod Years: 1985-date
Prod Numbers: Approx 210
For: Excellent chassis, Jag power makes it a delight to drive, superb quality, highly accurate, you don't even get wet in the SS
Against: LM is by nature impractical, all are very expensive
Verdict: One of the well-trusted leaders of the replica scene
Price Guide
A £25,000   **B** £18,000   **C** £9000
Current Maker: Ram Automotive, Maldon, Essex

Ranger

☆☆☆☆

Operating initially as EJS Products in Romford, and then from a disused cinema in Leigh-on-Sea, Essex, Ranger Automotive offered this Moke-style machine just as the fun car boom was dying - and made a good fist of it. Unusually, it used not Mini but BMC 1100/1300 parts, and that included both subframes, the dash, seats, windscreen and lights. Treated space frame chassis, pre-coloured GRP body with bonded-in plywood floor. Kits started at £245 and there were optional tops: estate hardtop, soft-top or pick-up cab. In 1976 Ranger Automotive was wound up but a modified revival in Wales occurred in 1984.

Prod Years: 1971-76/1984-85
Prod Numbers: Several hundred
For: Much lighter than an Austin 1100 so performance is fair, quite good-looking, bigger than a Moke, might be fun in the sun
Against: Drives like an 1100, rusty rear subframes, most are likely to be shabby grot-mobiles by now, long out of production
Verdict: Cheapie jeepie
Price Guide
A £1000   **B** £500   **C** £150
Current Maker: None

Ranger Cub

☆☆☆

This highly original three-wheeler was designed by Eric Salmons and Alan White of Ranger Automotive and made use of a Mini front subframe mounted in a square tube space frame chassis. The single rear wheel was suspended by half of the original Mini's suspension. Also used were the Mini's windscreen and lighting. Kits were cheap at £199 plus tax and sold well, even if the hood was an optional extra (as was the boot, which was omitted to keep weight below the 8cwt legal limit for three-wheelers). When Ranger died in 1976, it took down an electric prototype Cub and the four-wheeler (see below).

Prod Years: 1974-76
Prod Numbers: Approx 200
For: Original appearance, light weight, good handling, great fun, exceptionally cheap to run
Against: Pretty basic, wobbly glassfibre, poor engine access
Verdict: If you like cheap fun motoring, join the Cub
Price Guide
A £1400   **B** £900   **C** £400
Current Maker: None

Ranger Cub 4

☆☆☆

The Mini based Cub trike was doing so well for Ranger that they decided to do a more practical four-wheeled pick-up version. The Cub chassis was widened at the back to accommodate a standard Mini rear subframe and the bodywork chopped about, considerably extended and given a drop-down tailgate. Its debut was the 1975 Speedshow but, despite further exposure at the National Custom Car Show, Ranger never got into gear with production and ran into financial trouble in 1976. As such the four-wheeled Cub is one of kitcardom's real rarities, just four having been built.

Prod Years: 1975-76
Prod Numbers: 4
For: Quite pretty in a froggy sort of way, reasonably practical, cheap to run, easy to service
Against: Never properly developed so no weather gear ever offered, lack of doors hampers everyday useability
Verdict: Pick one up for peanuts
Price Guide
A £1000   **B** £600   **C** £200
Current Maker: None

Rat

★★

Prod Years: 1970-92
Prod Numbers: Approx 420
For: Bundle of laughs on a sunny day, it doesn't look like all the rest
Against: It's still just a buggy, so expect draughts, a bouncy ride, zero handling and purple metalflake paint
Verdict: Rat'll do nicely (groan)
Price Guide
A £1800   **B** £1000   **C** £400
Current Maker: None

Three men called Robert, Anthony and Trevor joined their names together to christen their car - the Rat. It was nothing other than a GP Buggy hacked about to look rather different. It was made by Fibre-Fab of Wokingham, Berkshire, and had a distinctive 'drooping' front, and usually rectangular headlamps. Initially SWB only, though standard Beetle floorpan version available from 1973. Anthony Hill emigrated in 1981 and the project was taken on by Tim Cooksey, who introduced a set of side mouldings and an optional squarish front. Latterly sold by Country Volks, which continued to picture the Rat in its literature.

Rawlson 250LM/164LM

★★★★★

Prod Years: 1982-date
Prod Numbers: Approx 12
For: Very attractive shape (if not an exact replica), space for 2+2, very high quality glassfibre
Against: Beetle basis on early cars was embarrassing
Verdict: An under-rated rarity, especially with Ford or Alfa power
Price Guide
A £8000   **B** £5000   **C** £2500
Current Maker: Tiger Racing, London

Although it was marketed by Kent-based Replicar, this under-rated Ferrari replica was conceived and made by Rawlson of Dover, the well-known race car and glassfibre experts. The first prototype was made as early as 1976 but the production version arrived in 1982, initially with the ignominy of VW Beetle basis, but a Jago chassis for Ford CVH power was made in 1983. Sharman marketed it from 1984, then it passed to Classic Replicars. A chassis for mid-mounted Alfasud engines was offered and new 1987 owners Western Classics renamed it 164LM. Final owners Tiger (qv) offered the 250LM with Golf power; with the option of Rover V8 and Porsche lumps.

Renegade

★★

Prod Years: 1970-76
Prod Numbers: Approx 200
For: Something of a smoothie for a beach buggy, usual fun quotient
Against: Quality was never up to much and most will now be in a terrible state, usual buggy bummers
Verdict: Break-away faction of the buggy boom era
Price Guide
A £1200   **B** £700   **C** £300
Current Maker: None

Unlike most buggies, which were straight rip-offs, the Renegade was a kosher licence-built version of a buggy made by Glassco Inc of California. It was built in the UK by PABC/Eresbug of London for a VW Beetle floorpan shortened by 15½in. The lines of the glassfibre tub were rather more flowing than the usual buggy style and boasted recessed headlamps and a curved (Ford Anglia) windscreen. Production was assumed by the Four Seasons Buggy Co from 1971, and by GP from 1975, though very few more examples were made after that as the mould's quality had deteriorated badly.

Renegade T

★★

Prod Years: 1973-74
Prod Numbers: 10
For: The novelty, you get four proper seats, rarity value
Against: Ant-eater profile, crude old VW mechanicals
Verdict: Watch out Penelope Pitstop
Price Guide
A £1200   **B** £700   **C** £400
Current Maker: None

In autumn 1972, the Four Seasons Buggy Company reached an agreement with Apal SA of Belgium whereby a set of Renegade buggy moulds was swapped for a set of Apal Auki moulds. What's an Auki? It was a strange mixture of street rod, buggy and sports car styles, based on an American design and was to become, in Britain, the Renegade T. A full four-seater, the T was based on an unshortened VW 'pan. First shown at the January 1973 Racing Car Show, basic kits cost from £190, rising to £895 for a fully-built car. A four-door hardtop was developed for the T but only one was made.

Replicar Type 35

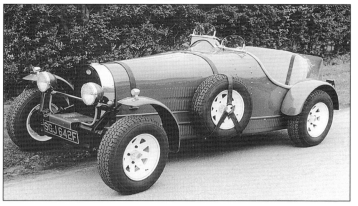

Alan Hatswell adopted a very successful American idea by plonking a glassfibre Bugatti Type 35 lookalike body on a cut-down Beetle floorpan. Kits were very cheap and the result looked great but the rear engine was as wrong as you could be. Supplemented by the Type 35c (with fold-able windscreen, hood and side screens) and Type 43 (see below). Kits were usually sold as basic body shells and quite a lot of work was needed to finish one; neverthe-less, many excellent examples were built. The project passed first to Chiltern Motors, then PBM, and finally (from 1992) to Lurastore of South London.

Prod Years: 1981-95
Prod Numbers: Approx 95
For: Encourages bally moustachioed japery, lots of fun (even with that banger in the back), cheap to run
Against: Basic weather gear (if any), not very practical, farty Beetle engine is a disgrace in this setting
Verdict: Try this one up Prescott and see the reaction
Price Guide
A £5000   **B** £3000   **C** £1300
Current Maker: None

Replicar Type 43

Replicar's Type 35 replica was going great guns but there was a special customer request for a more practical version with more than two seats. So Alan Hatswell developed the Type 43, which was essen-tially a Type 35 up to the end of the bon-net. Thereafter the glassfibre bodywork was modified by moving the windscreen forward and extending the cockpit towards the front. Hey presto, you had four seats! The nature of the modifications meant that kits were available to special order only, and the take-up was non-exis-tent. The '43' moniker recalls Bugatti's classic four-seater of 1927-31.

Prod Years: 1983
Prod Numbers: 1
For: Four seats is a welcome boost to practicality, should be cheap to run
Against: You lose 50% of the looks to get an extra pair of seats which are so small as to be virtually useless
Verdict: Buy a Type 35 instead
Price Guide
A £4000   **B** £2700   **C** £1300
Current Maker: None

Replicar SS100

A VW based SS100 replica getting four stars? Are they mad? Well, let us explain. Back in 1981, the standard of most kits left much to be desired and the SS100 market-ed by Replicar represented a great leap for-ward. Made by Antique & Classic Automotive of Buffalo, NY, its quality was very high, the proportions very pleasing (thanks to an extension of the Beetle chas-sis to bring the wheelbase up to that of an SS100) and the price was correspondingly high (kits started at £4000). At that price, not many kits were imported but they do make a good second-hand buy - if you can stomach the rear-mounted engine, that is.

Prod Years: 1981-84 (in UK)
Prod Numbers: 13 (in UK)
For: An elegant-looking machine, high quality of manufacture, four seats, cheap to run
Against: Beetle engine, check that the extended floorpan is still sound
Verdict: Surprisingly good for an old flat-four fun car
Price Guide
A £4000   **B** £2500   **C** £1300
Current Maker: None

Rhino

Before the Eagle RV, there was the Rhino. Brothers Don and Terry Mackenzie of Birmingham-based Eland Meres created a minor dynasty when they launched this jeep style device. The floorpan was unshortened Beetle (with repositioned driver's controls), the bodywork was in eight self-coloured glassfibre pieces and all major parts were taken from the Vee Dub. The Beetle wiring loom had to be modified and the front sus-pension softened. The boot was large and at the front (!). After a short production run, the Rhino project was bought by Alan Breeze's Eagle Cars who transformed it into the Ford based Eagle RV (see page 34).

Prod Years: 1981-83
Prod Numbers: 10
For: Large inside, four seats, GRP quality fair, cheap to run
Against: Beetle engine doesn't suit the style, fairly crude all round
Verdict: Uncle Sam's Jeep meets Herr Hitler's Kubel
Price Guide
A £1700   **B** £1100   **C** £500
Current Maker: None

Robin Hood Daytona

Prod Years: 1985-89
Prod Numbers: 70 (35 were SDI-based, and only 7 of these used modified SDI bodywork – rest are GRP)
For: Amazingly, it does look like a Daytona, quality is very good, stirring performance, good value
Against: May have rust problems, many areas not authentic
Verdict: Interesting route to Daytona
Price Guide
A £10,000   **B** £7000   **C** £4000
Current Maker: None

Robin Hood Engineering started life as a restoration company and moved towards the kit industry with an intriguing Ferrari Daytona replica. Pundits had always said the Rover SD1 aped its styling from the Daytona, and Robin Hood proved it by converting SD1 saloons into Ferrari replicas! The wheelbase was shortened and the Rover steel bodywork modified and the result was surprisingly convincing. Some customers spent up to £25,000 on these conversions – they were not strictly kits. Robin Hood moved into true kit form Daytonas with later GRP bodied Jaguar-based and Triumph TR7 based replicas – see Volume 4.

Rochdale Olympic Phase I

Prod Years: 1959-65
Prod Numbers: Approx 150
For: Neat appearance, potentially quite fast with the right engine, well-engineered and well-built, strong owners' club with good parts back-up
Against: Harsh ride, small interior
Verdict: One of the all-time classic kit cars, very collectable
Price Guide
A £3500   **B** £1800   **C** £800
Current Maker: None

Although Rochdale's attractive Olympic first saw the light of day as long ago as 1959, it stayed in production for a healthy stretch. Only the world's second all-glassfibre monocoque (after the Lotus Elite), it was a smart and well-engineered 'British Porsche'. The Phase I used Riley 1.5 or Ford side-valve engines, Riley IFS and coil sprung rear suspension. Most were two-seaters but some had very tight 2+2 seating. Phase I Olympics differed from later Phase II cars by their fixed rear windows and smaller bonnets. With 66bhp, expect 100mph and 0-60 in 12secs.

Rochdale Olympic Phase II

Prod Years: 1963-68
Prod Numbers: Approx 250
For: More practical and quicker than Phase I, classic shape, very well made for its era, attractive ownership prospect
Against: Not very spacious, typical crudities of the period
Verdict: Justifiably highly regarded
Price Guide
A £4000   **B** £2200   **C** £1000
Current Maker: None

With the Phase II, Rochdale moved the growingly popular Olympic into much more sophisticated territory thanks to its opening rear hatch, new dash and larger bonnet (which improved engine access no end). Mechanical improvements included Triumph Spitfire front suspension and disc front brakes. Most common engine is the Ford Cortina GT (78bhp, 114mph, 0-60mph 11.4 seconds), although Ford Anglia, Riley and MGA/MGB engines can also be found under the bonnet. Kits offered until 1968, though bare bodyshells continued to be made for many years after that.

Sabre Sprint

Prod Years: 1984-86
Prod Numbers: Quite a few
For: Rust-free body, four seats and a hatch, fairly roomy inside, Mini basis means cheap to run
Against: Boxy (non-)styling, poor GRP quality, rough finish, repair problems with a monocoque
Verdict: Like a non-rusty old Metro
Price Guide
A £1200   **B** £700   **C** £200
Current Maker: None

When the Sabre Sprint was launched, it was applauded for offering kit-built competition for the likes of the Mini Metro. Good though the concept might have been, the reality wasn't up to much. Conceived by a Newcastle firm which made GRP sunbeds, it was a Mini-based, glassfibre four-seater with a block-like nose, oblong headlamps and a glass tailgate. The Mini front sub-frame was used untouched in the monocoque but the rear one was swapped for a steel crossmember. Later examples had twin circular headlamps and modified rear end treatment with a full bumper-level GRP hatchback.

Sabre Vario

☆☆

If the Sabre Sprint was ugly, the Vario was positively Frankensteinian, which was a shame because at least with the Vario you could take the top off and have some fun. The Vario was basically a Sprint – all GRP monocoque body/chassis unit with Mini donor parts – with a clever interchangeable rear roof section: it could be lifted off, leaving a fixed front half. You lost the hatchback practicality of the Sprint, being supplied instead with a conventional hinging boot; however, you could take the bootlid off and replace it with a hatchback estate roof section in a matter of minutes, or so said the manufacturers.

Prod Years: 1985-86
Prod Numbers: Very few
For: Adaptable layout allowing the possibility of semi-open top motoring, Mini basis is advantageous
Against: It looks like a reject from a 1970s BL prototype shop, fairly crudely put together
Verdict: Vario-tion on a theme
Price Guide
A £1300   **B** £800   **C** £250
Current Maker: None

Sandbach Replica Cars

☆☆

From its base in Cheshire, Sandbach Replica Cars imported various kits from the USA, the most popular of which was undoubtedly the MG TD replica (pictured). This was intitially available for a VW Beetle floorpan (yeuch) but Sandbach developed a chassis for Vauxhall Chevette suspension and a choice of Vauxhall or Ford engines - which were at least in the right place! They also adapted this chassis to fit the Saxon (an imported Austin-Healey 3000 replica) and the Duke (an imported SS100 replica). But kits were extremely expensive and it is very doubtful if more than a handful were ever imported to the UK.

Prod Years: 1983-84 (in UK)
Prod Numbers: Very few
For: Decent quality and usually quite highly specified, some replicas looked fairly authentic
Against: Chevette chassis never really proven, get your barge pole out for the VW based cars
Verdict: It's unlikely you'll ever find one – maybe just as well
Price Guide
Don't pay much
Current Maker: None

Sandwood/Sheldonhurst Speedster

☆☆☆

Terry Sands created the Alfachassis (replacement VW chassis) because he didn't like Beetle based kits, but then went and produced a Beetle-based kit! It copied the Porsche Speedster at a time when only the very expensive Belgian-made Apal was available over here. It boasted the usual recipe of a shortened VW floorpan and glassfibre repro body, which was of good quality for the time. Many accurate repro Porsche parts, and a flared-arch Californian which presaged DJ's own (they were Sandwood agents). Sandwood changed its name to Classic Reproductions; in 1984 Sheldonhurst took the company over.

Prod Years: 1983-86
Prod Numbers: A few
For: Reasonable quality, visually accurate, Beetle basis is fitting (for once), plenty of replica parts back-up
Against: Not a match for more recent Speedsters, likely to have deteriorated by now
Verdict: Early Speedster replica - probably better to go for a Chesil or Apal
Price Guide
A £5000   **B** £3000   **C** £1500
Current Maker: None

Sandwood/Sheldonhurst Cobra

☆☆☆

The first Cobra replica from Sandwood was the usual cocktail of Jag suspension and V8 power, and was not an exceptional replica in any way. When Sheldonhurst absorbed Sandwood in 1984, they pioneered the development of a backbone chassis for a Cobra, creating the first of the true budget Cobras. The mechanical basis was Ford Granada, and almost everything was taken from this donor. V6 or Rover V8 engines were recommended. Sheldonhurst bit the dust in 1986 and the only kit from their range which was saved was the Cobra - southern agents Brightwheel took it on (and for that convoluted story see Vol 4).

Prod Years: 1984-86
Prod Numbers: Quite a few
For: Quality of mouldings was fair enough, accuracy of body not in question, Granada parts should make it cheap
Against: Usual early Cobra replica faults (poor detailing, unconvincing chassis)
Verdict: One of its relatives (Brightwheel or Cobretti) would be a better bet
Price Guide
A £10,500   **B** £7500   **C** £4500
Current Maker: None

Sandwood/Sheldonhurst XK120

☆☆

Prod Years: 1984-86
Prod Numbers: A few
For: Pretty good glassfibre quality, body looked convincing enough, Jag mechanicals a boon
Against: Dreadful chassis (weak, flexible, crude), details never properly sorted
Verdict: There are other, better XK120 replicas to choose from
Price Guide
A £6000   **B** £3800   **C** £2300
Current Maker: None

Sandwood's next replica was an XK120 lookalike which was based on an American kit which, unexpectedly, used Datsun 240/260Z mechanicals. For the UK market Sandwood developed a box section steel tube ladder chassis for Jaguar XJ mechanicals, although by all accounts it was a rather sorry affair. The rear axle was narrowed Jag XJ, while the front axle was specially modified. When Sheldonhurst took the project over it improved things slightly, but only slightly, and no-one really mourned when Sheldonhurst went pear-shaped in 1986. Certainly the XK120 replica died a death, and others took up the challenge.

Scamp Mk1

☆☆☆☆

Prod Years: 1970-78
Prod Numbers: Approx 700
For: Simplicity, honesty, toughness, durability, practicality, cheapness, Mini-ness, laugh-a-minute-ness
Against: Noisy, draughty, leaky, bouncy, flappy, graunchy
Verdict: Primitive cool
Price Guide
A £2000   **B** £1000   **C** £300
Current Maker: None

Robert Mandry, based in Whitchurch Hill, Reading, was the man behind the amazingly successful Scamp, which first appeared in 1970. Its Moke-like construction was tough and hid the inevitable Mini subframes. The multi-tube welded steel chassis was clothed with aluminium panels and could be ordered in six-wheel, van, estate or pick-up styles, and with a virtually infinite number of wheelbase lengths from ultra-short to unfeasibly long. Kits cost just £175 at launch and required only the addition of the necessary Mini bits. The only modification was shortened Mini pedals. The Mini-Scamp became tremendously popular.

Scamp Mk2

☆☆☆

Prod Years: 1978-90
Prod Numbers: Approx 2000
For: Extremely tough and durable, very simple and very cheap to buy/run, no-nonsense approach for work or play
Against: All the visual charm of a shoebox, don't expect much comfort or sophistication
Verdict: Perfect for lugging straw bales or junk furniture
Price Guide
A £2000   **B** £1000   **C** £300
Current Maker: None

In a blaze of publicity (there was a full press launch, virtually unprecedented in the kit car industry), Robert Mandry launched his Mk2 Scamp in 1978. It was an all-new design with a similar method of construction (tubular semi-space frame chassis with aluminium body panels). Appearance was uncompromisingly boxy. Mini front subframe, Mini rear trailing arms. Options: gullwing hardtop (later conventional), soft top, extension for six wheels, or do your own thing. Taken over by Surrey-based Andrew MacLean in 1987, who continues to offer an updated Mk3 Scamp (see Volume 4).

Scorpion

☆☆☆

Prod Years: 1972-75
Prod Numbers: 11
For: Quite pretty, quality of the glassfibre was good, strong 'survival cell', very rare
Against: Gullwing doors are inadequate, Rallye Imp engine can be troublesome, monocoque repairs and parts are a problem
Verdict: Interesting but flawed coupe, best left to Imp devotees
Price Guide
A £2500   **B** £1200   **C** £800
Current Maker: None

Tom Killeen was a pioneer of monocoque design (he claimed to have made the world's first monocoque in 1950), and one of his specials, the Imp-based K18, formed the basis for the Scorpion. The bodywork was semi-monocoque glassfibre (with a tubular steel roll-cage surrounding the cockpit area, hence the high sills). Gullwing doors were a novelty but were poorly conceived, ill-fitting and leaky. The rear-mounted engine was a twin carb 998cc Imp Rallye unit developing 65bhp, good for 95mph. This Clan Crusader rival arrived at the wrong time and suffered under poor management. Revived as the Kestrel Scorpion (see page 60).

Scout

☆☆☆☆☆

This was yet another Mini-based Moke style kit but at least it had some interesting features. The bodywork was an all-steel monocoque and was available in both four-wheel and six-wheel versions. First launched as the TMC Scout by a company called Import Export of Spalding, Lincs, but given an ambitious new injection of cash in 1987 by a new firm called Automotive Engineering & Manufacturing (AEM), though the inevitable bankruptcy came the following year. A third owner, a Solihull-based firm called The Sun Motor Company, revived it briefly in 1990. For all the tortuous production career, quite a few were made.

Prod Years: 1983-85/1987-88/ 1990-91
Prod Numbers: Quite a few
For: Tough and well-made little design, standard Mini parts, cheap to buy and run, practical, four seats (or more in six-wheeler)
Against: Steel structure may have rust in it, crude as an everyday car
Verdict: Half-metal jacket
Price Guide
A £2200   **B** £1200   **C** £600
Current Maker: None

SETA/ZETA

☆☆☆

By 1976, most of the fun had gone out of the great fun car boom of the early 1970s. In short, this was the kit car industry's darkest hour and not the best time to launch a Beetle-based kit, especially one as ugly as Malcolm Wilson's SETA. Just about the only thing to be said in the SETA's favour was that it used the VW floorpan completely unmodified, and kits, while expensive (over £1000), came with wheels, carpets, roll cage, wiring, even a stereo as standard. The gullwing doors lifted on hydraulic struts. Renamed ZETA. The moulds were offered for sale in 1980, 1981 and 1982, but that was this kit's last.

Prod Years: 1976-78
Prod Numbers: Approx 6
For: Standard VW floorpan, thick glassfibre, all flat glass, the next door neighbours aren't likely to have one
Against: Looks like it came out of a Cornflakes packet, rear engine, huge and cumbersome doors
Verdict: From a different age of kit cars that's best forgotten
Price Guide
A £1000   **B** £600   **C** £400
Current Maker: None

Shark

☆☆☆

Irishman Derry Treacy succumbed to the lure of the lucrative beach buggy market in 1970 by modifying a GP shell. The changes were most effective and made the Shark a buggy best-seller in its ephemeral life on this planet. Recessed and cowled headlamps straddled a pointed nose, while the rear end was cut off sharply. From a base in London, Treacy Ltd offered the usual GRP shell for a shortened VW 'pan, and good quality, novel looks and low prices (£112 for a shell) encouraged customers to Treacy's door. He also made a Shark 'T' street rod kit from 1971 (but only two were sold).

Prod Years: 1971-72
Prod Numbers: Approx 300
For: You can't mistake this buggy for anything else, smooth looks, even 25 years on it's still a lot of fun
Against: It's still a pain in the arse as well, few good ones about
Verdict: Top-jaw buggy
Price Guide
A £1100   **B** £700   **C** £300
Current Maker: None

Sheen Imperator GTS

☆☆☆☆☆

Ambitious wine merchant Peter Sheen aimed to better Italian coachbuilders with his own sports car. The Robert Peel company made the aluminium bodies on a Hillman Imp floorpan. It was intended to sell a 70bhp Nathan-tuned version for £950 and a 105bhp 1147cc five-speed Paul Emery modified variant for £1200. Even the base version was claimed to be good for 118mph. Production bodies - only 44½in high - were to be made of GRP but Rootes was unco-operative about supplying parts, so only two aluminium cars were ever made, which seems a shame.

Prod Years: 1964-65
Prod Numbers: 2
For: Aluminium body, smooth lines, racing performance and handling
Against: Hard ride, nervous disposition, effective extinction
Verdict: An ultra-rare specialist sports car delicacy
Price Guide
Impossible to quote
Current Maker: None

Spirit SS

☆☆☆

Prod Years: 1983-87
Prod Numbers: Quite a few
For: Decent quality, quite a few had lavish amounts of money spent on them, Cortina-based ones at least sound OK
Against: Beetle based ones are a joke, gross and tasteless, probably overpriced, did they really think people thought of a Mercedes when they saw it?
Verdict: Same sham shame
Price Guide
A £4000   **B** £2250   **C** £1000
Current Maker: None

Calamity Kit makers Automotive Design (AD) were the original company to offer this 'replica' of the Mercedes SSK in the American Gazelle vein. That meant a VW floorpan and rear-mounted engine, but at least AD tried to better the idea with their own Cortina-based chassis which offered 2+2 seating. They then divested themselves of the project to Spirit Cars of London, who offered it for three years until Daytona Classics took it on in 1986, renaming it Gatsby. They lasted but a year. Kits were costly at over £2000 a throw and the whole gaudy thing just didn't fire the British public's imagination.

Squire

☆☆☆☆☆

Prod Years: 1984-93
Prod Numbers: Approx 20
For: Fabulously elegant styling, authentic ash frame construction, meticulously crafted and engineered, practical mechanicals
Against: Difficulty of finding one for sale, poor luggage space
Verdict: Justifiably sought-after
Price Guide
A £10,000   **B** £6500   **C** £4000
Current Maker: None

Produced between 1935 and 1936, the Squire was one of motoring's greatest lost causes, as only seven were made. However, a near-exact replica was created by restorer Phil Kennedy, albeit using a steel box section chassis and Cortina mechanicals (later Alfa Romeo or V8). Perhaps the car's most impressive feature was its antique body construction, using the traditional method of an ash frame and aluminium main panels (though topped off with glassfibre sculpted wings). You also got attractive 18in wire wheels. Only 16 were built by the original maker before it passed on in 1993 to a Devon firm.

SR1/SR2

☆☆☆

Prod Years: 1985-86
Prod Numbers: Very few
For: Not unattractive styling, superb glassfibre quality, it's a definite rarity
Against: VW basis harks back to car's origins in the late 1970s
Verdict: Superb quality could make this a great used buy
Price Guide
A £2700   **B** £1500   **C** £900
Current Maker: None

Roy Coates bought an early Eurocco (fastback but no rear three-quarter window) and acquired the rights to make it in 1982. After three years, it was ready to go on the market but by 1985 the idea of a VW based coupe was looking distinctly outdated and the car got few takers. That was a shame because Coates' workmanship was extremely impressive. SR1 was a two-seater, SR2 was 2+2. Unmodified VW floorpan or S & R Sports Cars' own space frame chassis. Kits were fairly expensive at £1650 plus VAT but then quality was very high. Used Audi Quattro headlamps, Sierra rear lights.

Stanbury TT

☆☆

Prod Years: 1983-86
Prod Numbers: A few
For: Honest uncompromising character, ultra simple, fun to pilot, cheap
Against: Complete absence of aesthetic line, zilch comfort, more exposed than a motorbike, absolutely no frills - just chills
Verdict: Stark as a stick
Price Guide
A £800   **B** £400   **C** £100
Current Maker: None

Female kit car manufacturers are rare indeed but Weston-super-Mare based Jan Quick was unusual in another way: she couldn't even drive until two years before making the Stanbury TT (from the drawing board of her husband Dave). Ultra-simple design used a Triumph Herald chassis (minus outriggers), plywood floor and bulkheads, aluminium-skinned wood body and aluminium cycle wings. Morris 8 wire wheels or Triumph steels/wires. A body kit cost just £250 or you could build one from scratch from plans. Later examples were improved somewhat.

Status Symbol/Minipower

☆☆☆☆☆

Ex-Lotus and Clan engineer Brian Luff set up Status Cars to sell a Mini-based space frame chassis, mostly to autocross drivers. Disgusted by the Lotus Seven S4 ("a crumpet catcher," he said), he made his own GRP body for the Status chassis: the Symbol resulted. Features included a right-hand mounted gear lever, independent double wishbone suspension all round, any BMC A-series engine driving through BMC 1100 driveshafts and soft and hard top options, the latter a bizarre rear-hinged canopy. The name was changed to Minipower in 1972. Of 20 chassis supplied, only 8 had Luff's bodyshell.

Prod Years: 1971-73
Prod Numbers: 8
For: Brilliant Formula 1-style space frame chassis, weighs only 9cwt (457kg) so excellent performance, superb handling, very low-slung styling
Against: Cramped cockpit, crude weather gear (if any), odd nose treatment
Verdict: Any car of which Colin Chapman said "This is how the Lotus 7 S4 should have been" must be worth a look
Price Guide
A £5000   B £3500   C £1500
Current Maker: None

Status 365

☆☆☆

Brian Luff's next project was the 365, so named because it was designed to be used every day of the year. The styling was a curious mix between Clan Crusader and Lotus Elite, not surprising since the stylist was John Frayling who had been involved with both these projects (Status's location in Norfolk meant lots of ex-Lotus employees). The glassfibre-and-wood bodywork seated four and featured odd three-piece front glass and a rear hatch - unheard-of practicality for a '70s kit car. The monocoque body sat atop Mini subframes. Luff remained a quiet player in the kit scene, going on to develop the Minus (see page 75).

Prod Years: 1974-81
Prod Numbers: Approx 40
For: Well engineered, reasonable quality, goes well, seats four plus luggage, unrivalled '70s styling (most were yellow too - wow!), all Mini parts
Against: Haywire proportions, silly side windows, crash repair problems of a monocoque
Verdict: Pretend it's a demented mini-Lotus Elite prototype
Price Guide
A £1000   B £700   C £400
Current Maker: None

Stevens Cipher

☆☆☆☆☆

Anthony Stevens began his manufacturing career making pioneering period-style vans on Escorts and Transits from 1972, then the Reliant-based Sienna prototype in 1976. That led to the 1980 Cipher, co-designed with Peter Bird. Reliant Kitten mechanicals were humble but the shape was spot-on. GRP panels hung on a separate steel frame, and the Cipher even passed crash tests. Some heralded it as the Frogeye Sprite reborn but finance never materialised for a production run. Instead, kits were offered from 1983 by Peter Bird's Falcon Design at £3500, including an all-new drive train. Sadly, it didn't last.

Prod Years: 1980-84
Prod Numbers: 8
For: Great engineering integrity (fully Type Approved), well made, amazingly economical, nice interior, practical ownership proposition
Against: Engine never did the car justice, very few were made
Verdict: One lost cause which is definitely worth looking out for
Price Guide
A £4000   B £2750   C £1600
Current Maker: None

Stimson Mini Bug 1

☆☆☆

The prodigious Barrie Stimson's first kit car was the Mini Bug which, as its name suggests, was a buggy based on Mini bits - the world's first, it was claimed. The style was certainly original, with the headlamp pods (reputedly moulded from a woman's bra) mounted just in front of the windscreen pillar. There was no lower bodywork to speak of. Underneath the shell lay a space frame chassis into which Mini subframes bolted. The floor was plywood, the shell naturally GRP. Kits cost £170 and extras included a wrap-around perspex windscreen (illegal, so make sure a later-style glass screen is fitted), plus a roll-over bar and hood.

Prod Years: 1970-71
Prod Numbers: Approx 20
For: Zany character, Mini bits give it some practicality and of course the usual Mini dynamics, weighs only 9cwt (450kg)
Against: Looks like it ought to float, crude in most ways, luggage space at a premium
Verdict: Once advertised as 'the ugliest car around' - no argument there
Price Guide
A £1100   B £800   C £500
Current Maker: None

Stimson Mini Bug 2

★★★

Prod Years: 1971-73
Prod Numbers: Approx 160
For: Totally original styling, a certain absurdity, should go like the clappers (it only weighs 9cwt)
Against: Darned awkward to get into, dratted uncomfortable ride
Verdict: Bug-eyed wonder
Price Guide
A £1100   **B** £750   **C** £400
Current Maker: None

Announced at the 1971 Racing Car Show, Stimson's follow-up Mini Bug was actually a 1½, as it featured bumpers instead of the fill-in front and rear panels, and no glassfibre windscreen surround. Three 1½s were built before the definitive Mini Bug 2 came on stream. Main differences over the Minibug 1 included smoothed-out styling, a lift-off one-piece front body and an optional GRP targa bar with perspex rear screen. Kits cost £170 and about half the total production was exported. Main claim to fame: crashing at the 1971 Monaco Grand Prix with Graham Hill's wife in the passenger-seat.

Stimson CS+I/CS+II

★★★

Prod Years: 1973/1975-77
Prod Numbers: 4/2
For: Looks like a sci-fi space pod, goes like a buzzbomb, corners like a train
Against: Rides like a cart, and the roll cage is intrusive
Verdict: Fast and feisty flea
Price Guide
A £1100   **B** £750   **C** £400
Current Maker: None

Autocross pilots had already discovered the joys of racing the outrageous Mini Bug, and an even wilder 'Competition Special' (CS) version was launched in 1973. It used the Mini Bug 2 bodyshell with a 3in wider cockpit, beefed-up chassis and roll cage. Barrie Stimson emigrated to France in 1973, just after launching the CS+I, so only four were made. On his return he marketed a road version called the CS+II for £340 plus VAT, but despite supplying a number of chassis he only made two CS+IIs before passing the project on to Mini Motors of Rochdale (see CS2, page 27).

Stimson Safari Six

★★★

Prod Years: 1972-73
Prod Numbers: Approx 20
For: Not bad looking, lots of space, practical and cheap to run, well-made, there's nothing else quite like it
Against: Very rare, most will have deteriorated under use and old age, not very sophisticated
Verdict: A surprisingly attractive alternative car package
Price Guide
A £1900   **B** £1100   **C** £600
Current Maker: None

Barrie Stimson's Safari Six of 1972 was quite innovative for the time: a modern six-wheeled Moke/buggy cross-over which used Mini mechanicals. The windscreen, wheels, instruments and seats also came from the Mini. The design was quite attractive, and there was space for four adults plus a pick-up type rear deck at the back. Full weather gear was also offered, including a zip-up sidescreen/door. Financial wrangles killed the project after only a year; a planned four-wheeled Safari Four never materialised. A Welsh company later planned a relaunch under the name Shikari but this came to nought.

Stimson Scorcher

★★★★★

Prod Years: 1976-81
Prod Numbers: Approx 30
For: Utterly unique style and character, weighing only 5cwt (250kg) it lives up to its name, hoot-a-minute fun, cheap tax, moulds still exist
Against: Top speed limited to 80mph by pressure on your chest, there is no more exposed way to travel, second-hand ones rarely come up for sale
Verdict: Phew, what a...
Price Guide
A £2000   **B** £1400   **C** £1000
Current Maker: None

If the six-wheeled Safari was weird, the three-wheeled Scorcher was positively barmy. In construction, it had a triangulated tubular steel chassis, a Mini front subframe and a GRP body. There the logic breaks down. The Scorcher looked like a playground horse and indeed the driver and two tandem passengers sat astride it. The Mini engine was utterly exposed (unless you bought an optional bonnet), while the clutch was separated from the brake and throttle pedals and the gear lever centrally sited. Was classified as a motorbike-and-sidecar! Kits cost £385 from Noovoh Developments of Brighton. Highly sought-after.

Stimson Trek

☆☆☆☆☆

Barrie Stimson's final fling before emigrating to Australia was just as unusual as his previous devices. Thousands of readers followed the genesis of the Trek in *Kit Car* magazine in 1981, and they could scarcely believe their eyes. It was sort of a four-wheeled Scorcher with a very tall roll-over cage and windscreen, although the two rear passengers sat side-by-side rather than in tandem. Overall the crazy Trek was extremely narrow and rather short too. Again the basis was Mini. Kits cost £924 and the options list included weather gear, boot and dash panel. Stimson sold out in 1983 to a firm called Sarronset.

Prod Years: 1981-85
Prod Numbers: Quite a few
For: More madcap style, very lightweight so performance is high, seats three (just), compact dimensions
Against: Skittery behaviour, not particularly well-made, rather exposed seating position, odd driving position
Verdict: More suitable for Star Trek than earth-bound treks
Price Guide
A £1000   B £700   C £500
Current Maker: None

Sylva Star

☆☆☆☆☆

Draughtsman Jeremy Phillips was behind the individual-looking Star, a sort of modern interpretation of the Lotus 7. The chassis was a tubular steel space frame affair with stressed sheet steel panelling, and glassfibre body panels fitted at either end. Unusually the Leader was designed around Vauxhall Viva or Chevette components, though engine options also included Ford crossflow and Fiat twin cam. The Vauxhall suspension, pedals and rear axle were all modified. Low kit prices meant competition for Dutton. Revised all-GRP Leader replaced it in 1984, from 1985 made by Swindon Sports Cars, then Robley Motors.

Prod Years: 1982-84
Prod Numbers: Approx 70
For: Excellent chassis well proven in competition, build quality far superior to the Duttons of the time, sharp handling, good value and lots of fun
Against: Viva engined ones are hardly exotic or fast, fairly crude as a road car, odd-looking styling
Verdict: Cheap fun for sunny days
Price Guide
A £3000   B £1800   C £700
Current Maker: None

Sylva Leader

☆☆☆☆☆

The Leader was the natural successor to the Star, though the latter remained in production. The severe wing line of the Star gave way to a rather more rounded shape, and the aluminium side panels became moulded GRP with built-in skirts. Space frame chassis was carried over except for steel sheeting under the GRP body sides for extra crash protection. Running gear was still Viva, but the drive train was more often Ford. Kits were more expensive at £1085 plus VAT; windscreen and weather gear were extra. Passed to Swindon Sports Cars in 1985, then Robley Motors, neither of whom made many.

Prod Years: 1984-91
Prod Numbers: Approx 150
For: Well engineered chassis, slightly better looking than the Star, reasonably well manufactured, good value
Against: Vauxhall axles limit ultimate handling, not very sophisticated
Verdict: Respected sportster
Price Guide
A £3000   B £1800   C £700
Current Maker: None

Teal Type 35

☆☆☆☆☆

When it first appeared in 1984, Ian Foster's Teal was only slightly a cut above other Bugatti Type 35 replicas in that it had a front-mounted engine (most replicas had Beetle floorpans). Very quickly it became probably the world's leading Type 35 replica, with the glassfibre bodywork swapped for beautifully hand-crafted aluminium and unsuitable wheels ditched in favour of highly suitable 18in wires. Four-seat Tourer version came in 1986, Type 44 arrived in 1988 (see Volume 4). Initially a twin rail chassis for Morris Marina parts, though other options included Nissan Silvia turbo and Triumph straight six.

Prod Years: 1984-date
Prod Numbers: Several hundred
For: Certainly looks the part (especially with 18in wire wheels), fine aluminium bodies on all but earliest cars, very high standards of manufacture
Against: Early ones are not 5-star cars, Marina components unsophisticated (though the antiquated suspension looks right!), very exposed cockpit
Verdict: Superlative vintage evocation
Price Guide
A £12,500   B £8000   C £4000
Current Maker: Teal Cars, Cheshire

TiCi

☆☆☆

Prod Years: 1972-73
Prod Numbers: Approx 40
For: Nippy, brilliant in city traffic, highly suitable for extroverts, great fun on a hot day, Mini bits
Against: Shoebox luggage space, poor engine access, cramped and uncomfortable, fragile monocoque
Verdict: Motorised roller skate
Price Guide
A £1000   **B** £600   **C** £300
Current Maker: None

Furniture design lecturer Anthony Hill made his first TiCi town car in 1969: a tiny (6ft long) Triumph Daytona powered microcar. The production TiCi (pronounced 'tichy') arrived in 1972. It was bigger (still only 89in long, though), and featured a striking glassfibre monocoque body design. Mini front subframe and engine in the rear, moulded-in seats for two, optional removable hardtop and solid doors. Described as a mid-engined city sprint commuter car. Financed by ex-BRM sponsor Raymond Mays, supported by Stirling Moss, six went to Spain, six to Japan and other buyers included Eartha Kitt, Showaddywaddy and Clive Sinclair!

TI Tuscan

☆☆☆

Prod Years: 1985-86
Prod Numbers: A few
For: Should be cheap if you find one, body looks convincing enough, Ford components make life easy
Against: Fairly basic on the development front, many detail inaccuracies, everyday Ford parts not really suited to a Cobra replica
Verdict: Obscure Cobra kit rarity
Price Guide
Probably £4000-10,000
Current Maker: None

Husband and wife Tim and Jackie Ivory (Tim was an ex-aircraft engineer) set up a professional kit build-up service in 1984 and branched out into Cobra replication in 1985, launching the Tuscan at Stoneleigh that year. It had a steel box section ladder chassis for Ford Cortina front suspension and Capri rear end, plus Capri brakes and unmodified steering column. This was still fairly early days for Cobra replicators, so the spec was not entirely authentic and a wide variation in build-ups was noted. TI Motors was based in Greenfields, Bedfordshire. There was too much competition for the Tuscan to last.

Tigress

☆☆

Prod Years: 1983-85
Prod Numbers: Very few
For: Substantial GRP bodywork, all standard VW bits, seats four (just), quite well put together
Against: Awkward styling, shame about the rear engine and floorpan, check for leaking doors
Verdict: If you can put up with the looks and Beetle power, it might make a novel choice
Price Guide
Probably around £1200
Current Maker: None

Scottish kit cars are thin on the ground, but it was surely not geographical remoteness which sealed the Tigress' fate: it was simply not all there. By the time it was launched (1983), VW Beetle based kits were going out of fashion and the fact the Tigress looked pretty weird did not help its cause. It had such refinements as unusual, Countach-style forward-hinging doors with winding Beetle windows, ready-painted GRP body and 2+2 seating. The floorpan was unshortened, though the handbrake and gear lever had to be resited rearwards and the steering column lengthened. Made by Autocult of Dunbar, East Lothian.

TMC Costin

☆☆☆☆☆

Prod Years: 1983-88
Prod Numbers: 26
For: Costin's chassis is one of the best so expect fantastic handling, potentially very high performance, well made, more comfortable and practical than the average Sevenesque roadster
Against: Ungainly appearance (especially from the rear), odd detailing, small doors
Verdict: Flawed masterpiece and a great lost cause
Price Guide
A £9000   **B** £7000   **C** £4000
Current Maker: None

Ace aerodynamicist and celebrated engineer Frank Costin was called in to do this interesting car by Peter Thompson of the Thompson Manufacturing Co (TMC), based in Castlebridge in Ireland. Costin's space frame chassis was superb, the independent front suspension and self-adjusting rear end worked fabulously, the Ford engines (84bhp 1600, 110bhp XR3 or 130bhp Cosworth BDR) were perky and roadholding miraculous. But the GRP/Kevlar/aluminium body was a let-down: the rear end was a hotchpotch of lines and the standard fixed hardtop looked ugly. You did get a targa hood and glass rear hatch, though.

Tornado Talisman

☆☆☆☆☆

After producing several hundred specials bodies (see forthcoming volume in this book series, on Fifties Specials), Bill Woodhouse's Tornado Cars moved up-market to the Talisman. The tubular steel ladder frame chassis used Ford 109E (1340cc) or 116E (1498cc) power, with optional Cosworth tuning - a historic milestone because this was the first-ever road car with a Cossie motor. One solitary example even had a Daimler SP250 V8 engine. Attractive GRP bodywork could seat two people with room for two children in the back. After the 1963 liquidation of the parent company, the Talisman never really recovered.

Prod Years: 1961-64
Prod Numbers: 186
For: Attractive shape, practical accommodation, well made and properly sorted, Cosworth ones are quick and highly sought-after (worth more)
Against: Hard to find, crude by today's standards
Verdict: Convincing specialist sports car with a good reputation
Price Guide
A £4000   **B** £2000   **C** £800
Current Maker: None

Tramp

☆☆☆☆

The Tramp was the very first design of Richard Oakes, then employed by Western Laminates of Brixham, Devon, who went on to make this original buggy. Of the few British buggies which were not plagiaristic, the Tramp was the only one to have any integrity. It was unusual-looking, with a very highly swept-up tail exposing the Beetle engine, and the quality of the glassfibre was way above the norm. Unlike most buggies, it also complied with Constructions & Use regulations. Designed for an unshortened VW floorpan. Oakes left Western Laminates early on and the Tramp was produced only while the buggy boom was in full swing.

Prod Years: 1970-71
Prod Numbers: Approx 75
For: Novel apperance, it's a Richard Oakes design, thick GRP, unshortened VW floorpan means no potentially lethal chassis faults, four seats
Against: At the end of the day it's just another ageing buggy
Verdict: A breath of fresh air in a world of buggy clones
Price Guide
A £1300   **B** £900   **C** £400
Current Maker: None

Trident Venturer

☆☆☆☆☆

Although it was very up-market, the Trident was a kit car. An ex-TVR design, brought to production by TVR dealer Bill Last, albeit modified with glassfibre bodies and Austin-Healey 3000 chassis. Into this he plonked a 390bhp Ford V8 (gulp) to make the Clipper (not a kit). The Healey left production in '68, so a lengthened TR6 chassis was then used. More sensible was the Venturer with Ford 3-litre V6 engine, first offered from 1969 on the TR6 platform only. Expensive at £1939 in kit form but very well equipped. Died in '74 but Clipper was briefly revived in 1976. Clippers worth 50% more than Venturers.

Prod Years: 1969-74
Prod Numbers: Approx 135 (all types)
For: Smart Trevor Fiore styling, good performance thick GRP bodies
Against: Rust underneath, never very well made, rather unrefined and underdeveloped
Verdict: A lot of presence, if not much raw ability
Price Guide
A £7500   **B** £5000   **C** £3000
Current Maker: None

Trident Tycoon

☆☆☆☆☆

Since all Tridents from 1970 used lengthened Triumph TR6 chassis, it made sense for Ipswich based Trident Cars to offer one of its own cars with a TR6 engine, especially as Ford were on strike at the time and unable to supply 3.0-litre V6 engines. This happened in 1971, and the result was the Tycoon, fitted with a 150bhp Triumph six and displaying a restyled nose. It also had standard automatic transmission. Trident went bust in 1974 and the Tycoon was not revived when the company reappeared under new sponsorship in 1976. As a result, a mere six examples were sold in total.

Prod Years: 1971-73
Prod Numbers: 6
For: 150bhp gives more raw performance than Venturer (though auto 'box is un-sporting), same beautiful shape
Against: Extremely rare, potentially rusty chassis, fit and finish are likely to be questionable
Verdict: Faded glory unlikely to be owned by tycoons
Price Guide
A £7000   **B** £4500   **C** £2500
Current Maker: None

Triking

Prod Years: 1979-date
Prod Numbers: Approx 135
For: Great shape which is not a slavish copy of a Morgan, the most amazing fun, very quick, sharp handling, only 7cwt (350kg), well engineered
Against: Expensive compared to other trikes, very tight cockpit, most were exported so finding one isn't that easy
Verdict: The original and best of the modern Morgan-inspired trikes
Price Guide
A £9000 **B** £6500 **C** £4000
Current Maker: Triking, Norwich

Draughtsman and Morgan trike fanatic Tony Divey was the first person to launch a modern-day kit re-interpretation of the Morgan. And a superb beast it was. The backbone space frame chassis carried stressed aluminium body panels plus a GRP bonnet, tail and cycle wings. Triumph-based steering and front suspension, swinging rear fork driven by shaft from a very exposed Moto Guzzi V-twin engine. In 844cc form, this delivered 68bhp; with 950cc 71bhp engine things got very exciting, while the ultimate 85bhp Le Mans engine gave 240bhp per ton! Linear 'bike 'box, optional Toyota 5-speed or auto, and snug hood.

Tripos R81

Prod Years: 1984-92
Prod Numbers: 6
For: Purpose designed suspension, brilliant chassis, race car handling, light weight, high standard of manufacture and finish
Against: Very exposed and cramped cockpit, noisy and unrefined, no boot space, extreme rarity
Verdict: One of the more tragic 'lost' kit cars
Price Guide
A £6500 **B** £5000 **C** £3500
Current Maker: None

Before everyone cottoned on to the bottomless Lotus 7 replica market, the Tripos had successfully updated the concept and was arguably better than the original. Why then did it not succeed? Perhaps a lack of identity, but probably indifferent marketing, unsurprising since the R81 was originally architect Laurie Abbott's one-off. First one was Alfa based but ASD's Bob Egginton applied Formula 4 principles to make a Ford-engined kit version. Double wishbone front suspension, five-link live rear axle, space frame chassis. New owners from 1992 were supposedly Cobretti, but no more was heard of the project.

Tripper

Prod Years: 1971-79/1983-84/1986
Prod Numbers: Approx 85
For: No other buggy or sports car looks like it (especially in lime green), can seat four, great name
Against: Let's face it - it's an ugly bugger of a car, potential rust in Triumph chassis, one of the most ridiculous roll-over bars in history
Verdict: Wibbly-wobbly left-over from the psychedelic era
Price Guide
A £1500 **B** £1000 **C** £400
Current Maker: None

Of no other car can it be said that it was born as the result of a stomach ulcer. Torix Bennett, son of the founder of Fairthorpe, was in hospital when he conceived the Technical Exponents (TX) Tripper. A collision of contorted curves, obscene bulges and wobbly bits, it was a kind of buggy/sports car crossover which used a Triumph Spitfire chassis. Some had Triumph 2.5 PI engines, or even a 152bhp TR6, in which case 125mph and 0-60mph in 6.4 seconds was possible. Kits cost £180 (£740 complete), while a hard top was optional. The Tripper was twice revived, in 1983 and 1986, though with no more success than one would imagine.

Turner 803/950 Sports

Prod Years: 1955-57/1957-59
Prod Numbers: 90/170
For: Cute shape, very light weight, simple Austin components, honest small sports car
Against: 803cc engine has just 30bhp, very basic transportation, almost all went abroad
Verdict: Turner thought of the Frogeye Sprite before Austin
Price Guide
A £5000 **B** £3500 **C** £2500
Current Maker: None

Jack Turner's first public offering was the A30 Sports (also known as the 803), an Austin A30 803cc powered sports car using a tubular ladder frame chassis. The Austin also provided its coil spring front suspension, gearbox and hydromech brakes, anticipating the Austin-Healey Sprite. Rear suspension was by trailing arms and torsion bars. Glassfibre bodywork kept weight low and potential speed high. The 950 had the same A30 Sports chassis and body (although now with tiny tail fins), but came with the A35's hydraulic brakes and 948cc engine (which could be tuned as high as 60bhp).

Turner Sports MkI/II/III

☆☆☆☆☆

The 1959 Sports was the definitive Turner, and brought bigger sales. Revised front and rear bodywork with cut-down fins, and a wide spread of power options (including A35, Alexander crossflow head, Climax 1098cc and 1216cc units up to 90bhp). Optional front discs. The MkII also had Ford Anglia/Classic/Cortina power options, in which case Triumph Herald front suspension was fitted; 75-90bhp Coventry-Climax options remained for 100mph motoring (examples with Climax engines are worth 50% more). The MkIII had a bonnet scoop and elliptical tail-lamps. Most Turner Sports went to the USA.

Prod Years: 1959-60/1960-63/1963-66
Prod Numbers: 160/150/100
For: Refined profile, very strong club following, Turner-Climax examples are very rapid, race-proven
Against: No frills, rather rare
Verdict: Convincing little sports car
Price Guide
A £6000   B £4000   C £2800
Current Maker: None

Turner GT

☆☆☆☆☆

Worried that the Sports might become unpopular, Jack Turner designed an all-new GT model for launch in 1961. Bodywork was all-GRP, the centre section being a GRP monocoque with a steel floorpan, while the front and rear ends had square-tube steel frames. Triumph Herald front suspension, Ford 1498cc Cortina, 1340cc Classic or Coventry-Climax engines, standard front discs. Sleek styling (by Jack Turner) was mostly successful but the GT was only ever built on an individual order basis at a time when the specials industry was undergoing a recession, so very few were sold.

Prod Years: 1961-65
Prod Numbers: 10
For: Pretty shape, rarity value, pretty quick with any engine
Against: Finding one, very noisy inside, vague steering
Verdict: A rather attractive British sports car also-ran
Price Guide
A £6000   B £4000   C £2800
Current Maker: None

TVR Grantura MkI

☆☆☆☆☆

Trevor Wilkinson produced about 30 assorted cars and chassis before the first definitive TVR: the Grantura. It was a dumpy glassfibre bodied coupe with tubular backbone chassis, VW torsion bar and trailing arm suspension, wire wheels, Austin-Healey drums, Ford Consul windscreen. Large choice of engines: Ford 1172cc sidevalve (with optional 56bhp supercharging), Coventry-Climax 1100/1200, BMC B-series (usually MGA) and Ford 105E. Wire wheels, BMC final drive, optional front discs from 1960 and the (rare) option of lightweight bodywork if you wanted to go racing.

Prod Years: 1957-60
Prod Numbers: Approx 100
For: Charismatic dumpy styling, kudos of the 'first of the line', light weight, well engineered
Against: Cramped interior, noisy, not all that fast
Verdict: Classic genesis TVR
Price Guide
A £5000   B £3500   C £2300
Current Maker: None

TVR Grantura MkII/IIa

☆☆☆☆☆

The 1960 Grantura MkII was easily recognizable by its tiny rear fins and a blister over each rear wheel arch (as well as the front arches). Same engine options as MkI except that Ford sidevalves were deemed too archaic and there was the addition of the Ford Classic 1340cc unit from 1961. Climax powered cars had rack-and-pinion steering. Front disc brake option, which became standard on MkIIa, which also may have the larger 1622cc MGA engine. These early sixties Granturas were slightly heavier than the original MkIs, but increasing engine power outputs compensated and performance improved.

Prod Years: 1960-61/1961-62
Prod Numbers: Approx 400
For: Distinctive style, solid engineering, high quality glassfibre, practical proprietary power plants, excellent handling, big owners' club
Against: Still noisy and cramped
Verdict: Much sought-after by keen TVR aficionados
Price Guide
A £4500   B £3300   C £2200
Current Maker: None

TVR Grantura MkIII

Prod Years: 1962-64
Prod Numbers: Approx 90
For: Specification more established than earlier Granturas, chassis is much superior, great fun to drive
Against: Nowhere near as practical to run as an MGB (but then TVR buyers aren't in the market for an MGB...)
Verdict: Much better all-round than earlier Granturas
Price Guide
A £4700   B £3500   C £2300
Current Maker: None

Development of TVRs had progressed in a very piecemeal way up until this stage, but the Grantura began to coalesce with the MkIII. The all-new chassis was stiffer and the wheelbase longer, though the overall length remained the same. All-independent suspension was by coil springs and wishbones, and you got front discs and rack-and-pinion steering. Some early ones still had Ford 109E and Climax engines, but the spec solidified around MGA or, from '63, MGB engines; overdrive option with the latter. Expect 100mph performance with MG power and acceleration to match.

TVR Mk3 1800S/Mk4

Prod Years: 1964-66/1966-67
Prod Numbers: 128/78
For: Steadily becoming more practical, 1798cc MG engine boosts performance, entertaining ownership prospects, quite collectable
Against: Hard-riding, noisy and cramped, not beautiful
Verdict: MG power matures the Grantura into a decent '60s sports car
Price Guide
A £4700   B £3500   C £2300
Current Maker: None

The fins which had appeared in 1960 were removed again on the 1964 1800S, which boasted a distinctive new cut-off tail with circular Ford Cortina rear lights. The spare wheel was now sited above the floor rather than upright behind the rear axle. 1798cc MGB now the standard engine. TVR went bust in 1965 but was rescued by Arthur and Martin Lilley, who developed the confusingly-named Mk4 1800S, introduced in 1966. This was basically the same MGB-engined car, with identical bodywork to the Mk3, but had standard steel wheels, better trim, a larger tank and a tuned 115bhp engine option.

TVR Vixen S1

Prod Years: 1967-68
Prod Numbers: 117
For: Ford engine provides power and reliability, light weight means good performance, still fine handling, better made too
Against: Usual TVR discomforts
Verdict: Attractive proposition from many points of view
Price Guide
A £5000   B £3500   C £2000
Current Maker: None

The new name for the 1967 Grantura replacement was Vixen. The Lilleys' preference for Ford power starts to show, as the spec standardises around the 88bhp Ford 1600cc Cortina GT engine and fully synchronised gearbox (though even now, 12 early cars could not let go of MGB power). Externally, it all looked very familiar TVR stuff, apart from a new bonnet scoop. Steel wheels were standard and the option of wires was supplemented by alloys. There was less power but also less weight, so performance was still excellent: You can expect 106mph top speed and 0-60mph acceleration in 11 seconds.

TVR Vixen S2/S3/S4

Prod Years: 1968-70/1970-72/1972-73
Prod Numbers: 438/168/23
For: Now even better built and more comfortable, getting faster all the time, S4 has the better chassis, plenty around to choose from
Against: Hard-riding as ever
Verdict: Most refined of the old-school TVRs
Price Guide
A £5000   B £3500   C £2000
Current Maker: None

With the Vixen S2, TVR moved up to the longer Tuscan SE-type 90in wheelbase and substituted bolted-on bodywork instead of bonding (which certainly helps restoration). Also new was a standard brake servo. S3 of 1970-72 has standard alloy wheels, a 92bhp Capri 1600 engine and Zodiac MkIV square side vents. The 1972 S4 was an interim model with an all-new and much stiffer 2500M chassis but the old-style bodywork. Front track was wider on the S4. TVR made the headlines when nude models draped themselves over Vixens at successive Motor Shows. How times have changed.

TVR Tuscan V6

The first TVR to bear the Tuscan name was the mighty V8 successor to the legendary Griffith - but neither of these models was offered in kit form. However, the milder Tuscan V6 was (at a bargain £1492). It differed from its V8 relatives by its Vixen body and, of course, its 128bhp 3-litre Capri V6 engine. A significant option was dual overdrive, and the differential was similar to the Tuscan V8. Cast alloy wheels standard. Performance was nothing like the monstrous V8-powered Tuscans but was notably better than the Vixen, offering up to 125mph and 0-60mph in just 8.0 seconds.

Prod Years: 1969-71
Prod Numbers: 101
For: Very practical yet powerful Capri power, excellent performance, magical Tuscan name
Against: Not a common sight, not particularly favoured in TVR circles, bone-jarring ride
Verdict: Appealing and very rapid '60s TVR
Price Guide
A £6500   **B** £4500   **C** £3500
Current Maker: None

TVR 1300/2500

Under Martin Lilley, TVR supplemented its traditional Ford powered Vixen by courting Triumph. The 1300 was an economy special with a Spitfire engine, while the 2500 had a TR6 engine and gearbox (a move to get around US emissions regulations). The 1300 is now virtually non-existent (probably all re-engined), but the 2500 was successful. Structure and body were regular Vixen, though the last examples of both types had the M type chassis (just like the Vixen S4 which arrived just after these models). If you want a TR-engined TVR but like the earlier body style, this is for you.

Prod Years: 1971-72
Prod Numbers: 15/385
For: Healthy TR6 power (usually 150bhp) means brilliant performance (115mph), balanced handling
Against: 1300 is a poor performer but you're unlikely to find one anyway
Verdict: An eminently satisfying sports car package
Price Guide
A £6000   **B** £4000   **C** £2700
Current Maker: None

TVR 2500M

Although the new TVR M series chassis had already made its appearance in the last 1300/2500s and Vixen S4, the first true 'M' car was the 2500M. Over the stiffer 90in wheelbase chassis sat a new, longer body (still in glassfibre and with only two seats). The 2500M had a smog-restricted 106bhp TR6 engine/gearbox (though UK cars will have much more healthy 150bhp), front discs, standard alloys and optional overdrive. It was intended mainly for America, although complete cars and kits were sold in Britain too at prices from under £1800 (no purchase tax being payable on kits).

Prod Years: 1972-77
Prod Numbers: 947
For: TR6 engine makes life easy, interior much more roomy, body looks much more mature though it's still classically TVR
Against: Hard to find in the UK, avoid weedy US-spec cars
Verdict: Not as well liked as Ford-engined M series cars
Price Guide
A £5000   **B** £3500   **C** £2500
Current Maker: None

TVR 1600M

While the 2500M looked after America, the 1600M was mainly targeted at British customers, who indeed bought most of them. Under the bonnet sat a cooking Ford Cortina GT power train, which developed 86bhp and provided a top speed of 105mph and a claimed 0-60mph time of 10.5 seconds, while at the same returning a healthy 30+mpg. A lot of kits were sold but TVR decided to axe the 1600M in 1973 when VAT was introduced. However, it returned again as a useful economy model in 1975, although by this stage kits were a thing of the past for the famous Blackpool marque.

Prod Years: 1972-73/1975-77
Prod Numbers: 148
For: Decent performance and good fuel economy, very practical to run, better interior
Against: Not the most comfortable car to drive
Verdict: Appealing, though later 3000M is a better all-rounder
Price Guide
A £6000   **B** £4000   **C** £2800
Current Maker: None

TVR 3000M

☆☆☆☆☆

Prod Years: 1972-79
Prod Numbers: 654
For: Excellent performance, usual fine handling, easy serviceability, strong following, big owners' club
Against: If you're coming to it from a soft Capri, you'll find it hard to live with – small doors, noisy etc
Verdict: All the character and feel of a true British specialist sports car
Price Guide
A £6500   **B** £4500   **C** £3000
Current Maker: None

The 3000M shared its body and chassis with the other two members of the TVR M family but mixed into the brew that classic British power plant, the Ford Essex 3.0-litre V6, taken from the Capri (therefore 138bhp, top speed of 130mph and 0-60mph in 7.5 seconds). Optional overdrive improved touring economy, which was decent anyway thanks to light weight. It was a popular sports car in Britain, but only marginally a kit car: after 1973, TVR concentrated on selling cars fully-built, a job at which it proved to be extremely successful. TVR's survival of the oil crisis was down to the success of the M series.

Unipower GT

☆☆☆☆☆☆

Prod Years: 1966-70
Prod Numbers: 75
For: Extremely nimble handling, Cooper 'S' powered ones are very fast, pretty shape, good quality means high survival rate
Against: Cramped cockpit, notoriously difficult to get in and out of, noisy, rarity means high prices
Verdict: A1 collectable Mini special classic – if you can find one
Price Guide
A £9000   **B** £6000   **C** £3500
Current Maker: None

Probably the best of the many Mini-based sports cars of the 1960s was the Unipower. Designed by BMC works driver Andrew Hedges and Tim Powell, it was made by fork-lift manufacturer Universal Power Drives (hence Unipower). Mini-Cooper or Cooper 'S' engine mounted just ahead of rear axle in tubular space frame, to which the glassfibre body was bonded. Right-hand gearchange, front discs. Only 40in high, so getting in was an art-form. Fabulous handling and high performance (up to 120mph) due to light weight (½ton/570kg). Japan has sucked most of them away and they are nowadays a very rare sight.

UVA Fugitive

☆☆☆☆☆

Prod Years: 1984-date
Prod Numbers: Approx 500
For: Extremely simple, very tough chassis, purity of concept, with the right suspension makes a great off-roader, can be made to handle and perform amazingly well
Against: Just about the crudest drive around, avoid amateur V8 conversions (of which there are some)
Verdict: No-frills fun - shame there aren't any deserts in Britain
Price Guide
A £3000   **B** £1700   **C** £750

The idea of the 'sand rail' is pure American and UVA, as an importer of VW upgrade parts, was one of the first on the scene in the UK. UVA's Fugitive could be a pure off-roader or aimed towards road use, in which case it was a possible Caterham rival - even with the rear-mounted VW engine, it was a driver's car thanks to its very tough chassis and extreme light weight. With no interior trim (just plain metal panelling) and the absolute minimum of GRP bodywork, it was as stark as they come but tremendous fun. Four-seater option. Kit prices were extremely low. UVA went bust in 1991 but the 'Fugi' was revived.

UVA F30

☆☆☆☆☆

Prod Years: 1985-92
Prod Numbers: 4
For: Completely bonkers performance, radical appearance, tenacious road behaviour, corking (not to say frightening) fun, well engineered
Against: About as practical as a motorised roller-skate, hope you like flies in your teeth, sir
Verdict: A more single-minded motor car does not exist
Price Guide
A £6000   **B** £3000   **C** £1200
Current Makers: None

It was the (unwise) fitment of rear-mounted Rover V8 engines into Fugitives that led Alan Arnold of UVA to design a proper mid-engined version intended for that power plant. The absolute minimalist F30 was the result: styling was very similar to the Fugitive but a new space frame chassis was created for mid-mounted power, meaning the passengers sat further forward. The suspension remained VW-based, however. In 1986 came the F33 Can-Am, the definitive mid-engined Fugitive. It had much more enclosed bodywork on the same chassis, and is fully described in Volume 4.

UVA Montage

☆☆☆☆☆

The Montage McLaren M6GT replica originated in America with Manta Cars and was initially imported to, then manufactured in, Britain by The Unique Vehicle & Accessory Co (UVA). In its original VW Beetle based guise it obviously had a short shelf-life, so in 1986 UVA reworked the entire package to create the M6GTR after just seven VW kits had been sold. Now there was a GRP monocoque centre section with tubular steel front and rear subframes, designed to accept the Rover V8 engine and VW transmission. The body was also tweaked to make it look more modern. Sadly the sleek M6GTR was a casualty of UVA's financial trouble.

Prod Years: 1981-86 (in UK)
Prod Numbers: 7
For: All-time classic of exotic styling, top quality engineering and high manufacturing standards
Against: Not much space inside, Beetle-based ones are a let-down and tend to be shabby
Verdict: The alluring shape is hard for the heart to resist, and the UVA is also a choice your head will understand
Price Guide
A £16,000   B £10,000   C £5000
Current Maker: None

Vanclee

☆☆☆☆☆

Belgium has not turned up many great motor manufacturers, and I'm afraid that Vanclee was not among them. However, it did have the wonderful name of Vanclee Mungo (other names were Rusler and Emmet). A firm based in Belfast obtained a licence to make them and so this bizarre kit came to our shores with the name Vanclee Land Ranger. The basis was 2CV - some were supplied with brand new Citroen chassis - and the bodywork (in glassfibre) was a very simple and pretty ugly pick-up style. Options included a removable rear hardtop, soft top and solid GRP or soft vinyl doors. The project passed to Dutton and then JPR.

Prod Years: 1983-92 (in UK)
Prod Numbers: Quite a few
For: 500kg carrying capacity, amazing ride, cheap to buy and run, durable
Against: No effort was spared by the designer to uglify his creation, brick-like aerodynamics mean extreme sluggishness, very little 'cool'
Verdict: Why buy one of these instead of a Citroen Mehari?
Price Guide
A £1700   B £1000   C £600
Current Maker: None

Viking Minisport

☆☆☆☆☆

This ugly little bugger began life on the Isle of Man under Peel Engineering, better known for its minute three-wheelers. One Mr Kissack designed a car which the company called the Peel Trident Mini, which used Mini subframes in a square tube steel chassis. This was clothed in a GRP body fitted with a Mini windscreen and modified glassfibre Mini doors. Launched at the 1966 Racing Car Show, only two examples were made before Bill Last of Surrey-based Viking Performance assumed production and renamed the car the Viking Minisport. Last's involvement with the ex-TVR Trident led to him abandoning production in late 1966.

Prod Years: 1966
Prod Numbers: Approx 25
For: 2+2 seating, simple Mini bits, you'll certainly get attention
Against: It's probably going to be the wrong kind of attention 'cos it's a bulbous heap of plastic
Verdict: Bizarre contraption best left to collectors of Mini curiosities
Price Guide
A £1000   B £600   C £250
Current Maker: None

Viking

☆☆☆☆☆

Jaguar specialists Classic Cars of Coventry (where Lee Noble worked) conceived the Viking, whose name echoed an old Coventry car maker. Designer Peter Morris was inspired by the pre-war SS100, though it was not a copy. Into the box section chassis fitted Jaguar XJ6 suspension and any Jag XK six-cylinder power train. The bodywork was made from aluminium (the swoopy wings were glassfibre), while there were plenty of chrome-on-brass items. Kit prices were high at £6750. A breakup of the original team (operating from a factory in Blaby, Leics) led to another firm called Leaping Cats offering the same car.

Prod Years: 1980-83
Prod Numbers: Approx 8
For: Jag mechanicals, aluminium main bodywork, well engineered
Against: Not the prettiest traditional shape, very few around
Verdict: Sometimes described as a 'poor man's Panther J72'
Price Guide
A £8000   B £5500   C £3000
Current Maker: None

Left: This is the first production Lotus Seven from 1957, the stuff of legends. Below: About 350 Elva Courier MkIIs were made between 1959 and '61. They're now desirable classics.

Right: Ginetta's G2 of 1958 was the Essex company's answer to the Lotus Seven.
Below: Fairthorpe's early '60s Electron Minor sold well before being superseded by the less popular TX-GT (below right).
Bottom: One of the great barmy kit cars, the outrageous Opus HRF.

Above: Classic 1964 Marcos was famous both for its futuristic styling and original wooden chassis. It's one of the all-time great kit cars. Below: 1963/64 Deep Sanderson is a real rarity. This stretched example was built for racing at Le Mans.

Right: Tiny Mini-Cooper engined Unipower GT demonstrates its 40" height against Ford Cortina. Below: Elegant G15 became Ginetta's best seller between 1967-1973. Below right: Early '70s Jeffrey J5 reinterpreted the Seven theme. Bottom: Lovely Trevor Fiore styling graces desirable Trident Venturer made between 1969 and '74. Yes, it was a kit car!

Left: Wild looking, Imp powered Centaur was a mere 37" high. Only 26 were made. Below: Speedster replicas ultimately became kit market favourites. This is an early VW based Sheldonhurst example.

Right: Early Dax Cobra replica. This model went on to become the most famous of them all. Below: Another big favourite, the Spartan appeared in 1973. Below right: Like Spartan, Moss Roadster was originally Truimph Herald based. Bottom: Ford 3-litre V6 engine gave the classic Gilbern Invader (1969-72) smooth torquey power.

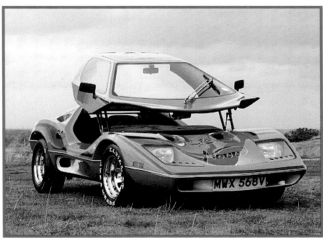

Left: MG's famous TF inspired the popular Gentry launched in 1973. Below: Richard Oakes styled the wild Nova with lifting cockpit canopy and VW Beetle basis.Bottom: Dutton was the biggest kit car maker of the 1980s with this trio of low cost roadsters. Inset: Avante, another Beetle based exotic.

Right: Launched in '97, the Marlin Roadster went on to be a real evergreen. Below: About 400 Beetle based, gull-wing doored Chargers were made. Below right: GP Madison was popular in early 1980s. Bottom: William Towns' Hustler was another early '80s favourite – this is a Huntsman.

Seaspray (1971) Rip-off of the Manta Ray (qv).

Seraph Sports Racer (1984-85) Before Seraph took on the ex-AED Bonito, it made an agressively styled, wedge shaped Ford mid-engined coupe with spaceframe chassis, probably only one of which was ever made *(pic 1)*.

Sheffield Beach Buggy (1970) A buggy made in... Sheffield.

Shepherd (1985-86) Ridiculous cardboard cut-out utility estate on Cortina parts with plywood body. Surely only one was ever made? *(pic 2)*.

Siva Sierra/Mehari (1976) Built as the sunset of Siva, Neville Trickett's jeep-type utility Sierra on Escort 1300 parts sold just three examples, while his Citroen Mehari replica was even more abortive.

Stallion (1985) A chap called Steven Povey made this extraordinary looking Jaguar-based four-seat tourer; the less said about it, the better *(pic 3)*.

Starborne Speedster (1978) This was the UK's first ever Porsche Speedster replica, actually imported from Apal in Belgium by Tim Dutton. But at £5000 no-one gave a hoot about it *(pic 4)*.

Sunlit (1983-84) Italian-designed GRP coupe body for Fiat 500/126 basis. Quickly became obscure.

Swift KJ280 (1983-85) John Swift designed this pleasant-looking and substantial aluminium-bodied roadster, intended for Ford Granada power. At £12,500 in complete kit form, it was too expensive to have any impact *(pic 6)*.

Trakka Trouper (1984) Renault 4 based jeep/utility car made by a company called CL Cars of Salford, Manchester, at prices from £650 plus tax *(pic 5)*.

UFO (1970-71) Outer space range of psychedelic buggies from a company in Birstall, Leics. Also offered the Doodlebug VW panel kit conversion.

UVA Shogan VW specialists and Fugitive/Montage kit makers UVA offered this kit/conversion cross-over in the early '80s: a glassfibre estate rear end for the VW Beetle. Quite a few were made *(pic 7)*.

Volksparts Basingstoke company made a couple of 1930s style GRP tubs for VW floorpans.

Westminster (1968-70) This was a very early Neville Trickett-designed GRP shell for Bentley MkVI chassis.

WH Imp (1970) Designed by Warwick University students Richard Haste and Tony Whitehead, the WH Imp was a squat, Imp based thing. Production reached 3.

Wild Blood In 1983, details of planned production of a Bugatti Type 55 replica were published but it never began; neither did that of an Austin A35-based Bugatti Brescia replica.

York 427 Early '80s Cobra replica which is very obscure.

Zigclair (1981) Gorgeous looking MGB-powered vintage Riley-style roadster which sadly never made production *(pic 8)*.

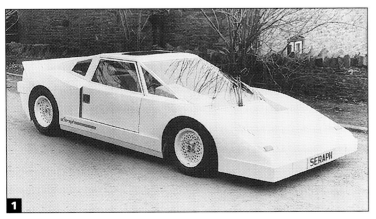

Cross-Reference Index

The main entries in this book are arranged by alphabetical order. Entries are arranged by the name of the company making the model, then by model in chronological order. Where more than one company made a particular model, it is listed by model name in alphabetical order. The cross-reference listing below identifies which companies made those models whose production careers took them through more than one manufacturer. It also shows which models were known by alternative names, and directs the reader to the more common usage listed in the book.

AF Spider - see AB1/AF Spider
ACM - see Bonito
ADD - see Nova
AED - see Bonito
AEM - see Scout
ACM - see Bonito
Amplas - see SN1 and Pulsar
Autobarn - see Gecko
Autocult - see Tigress
Bespoke - see Dingbat
Birchall - see McCoy
Bohanna Stables - see Nymph
Briton - see Kestrel and EWM
B&S - see EWM
Cartune - see Apal
Centaur - see Concept
Chiltern - see Replicar
Chimera - see AD 400
Cipher - see Stevens
Classic Cars of Coventry - see Viking
Classic Replicars - see Rawlson
Classic Reproductions - see Sandwood
Country Replicars - see Replicar
Cox - see GTM
CVC - see Bedouin
CW Autos - see Bugle
Delta - see Amica *
Del Tech - see Foers
Dorian - see Burlington SS
Dwornik - see Vincent Brooklands/MPH
Eagle - see Badsey *
Eland Meres - see Rhino
Embeesea - see Charger and Eurocco
Fellpoint - see Minijem and Futura
FES - see Kestrel
Fordham - see Daytona
Fugitive - see UVA
GDXM - see Griffin
Glenauld - see Helian

GPB - see Teal Type 59
GT Mouldings - see Baja, Bugle, Manta Ray, Kyote,
Hampshire Classics - see Moss
Hawk - see Wyvern
Heerey - see GTM
Highlander - see Jimini
IFS - see Kestrel
Innes Lee - see Scorpion
ISS - see Kestrel
JC - see Wyvern
Jet - see Albar
Kennedy - see Squire
Kimble - see MCA
Lakes - see Voyager
Lalande - see GP Centron II
L&R - see Ram
Laser - see UVA
Leaping Cats - see Viking
Lemazone - see SN1, Beaujangle and Amplas Pulsar
Lightspeed - see Magenta
Lurastore - see Replicar
MBC - see Charger
McLean - see Nimbus
MDB - see GP Centron II
Mini Motors - see Stimson
Minion - see Imperial
Mini-Scamp - see Scamp
MR - see Pulsar
Nomad - see Foers
One-Six-Two - see Albar
Pageant - see Amica *
Paris - see Merlin
Pastiche Henley = NG TF
Pastiche Ascot = NG TF
Pastiche Gladiator = NG TC V8
Peel - see Viking Minisport
Peerhouse - see Alto
Perry - see AD
PBM - see Replicar
Phoenix - see Gazelle
Primo - see GTM

Proteus - see Copycats
Projects of Distinction - see Teal
Pulsar - see Amplas
RMB - see Gentry
Robley - see Sylva
RW - see Karma
S&J - see Milano
Sarronset - see Stimson Trek
Saturn/Saratoga - see GP Centron II
Seraph - see Bonito
Shadow - see Kingfisher Mouldings Vulcan *
Sharman - see Rawlson
Sonic - see Apal
SP - see Gentry
Spectra - see NG/Speedwell *
Speedsters - see Apal Speedster
Steaney - see SN1
Sun - see Scout
SVC - see Specframe
Swindon Sports Cars - see Vincent Brooklands/MPH
TA - see NG TA
TAG - see UVA Fugitive
Talon - see GP Talon
TM - see Gentry
TMC - see Scout
TPC - see Apal Speedster
Trident Autovet - see AD
Tuscan - see TI
TX - see Tripper
Unique Autocraft - see Python
Vortex - see Kingfisher Sprint
Western Classics - see Rawlson
WV - see O&C
Wynes - see McCoy
Yak - see Grantura
YKC - see Marlin Roadster/Berlinetta
Zagaroff - see Silhouette
Zeta - see Seta

* Listed in *You Might Also Find*

The Filby Files Series

Illogical as it may seem, Volume 2 was in fact the first book to be published in the above series! Scheduled for publication between late 1997 and late 1998, the remaining volumes are as follows:

Volume 1 – A comprehensive guide to GRP and aluminium bodied production 'specials' and historic kit cars from 1948 to 1965. Detailed and illustrated is every known car from that period, including AKS, Ashley, Autobee, Buckler, Cannon, Convair, Dante, Diva, EB, Elva, Fairthorpe, Falcon, Heron, Hamblin, LMB Debonair, Microplas, Nickri, Peel, RGS, Rochdale, Speedex, Terrier, Tojeiro, Tornado, Turner, early TVR, Watford etc. Over 170 different cars in total. *Planned publication date: June 1998.*

Volume 3 – Covers every known British specialist sports car built as a protoype or for production and offered, or intended to be offered, in turn-key form. Includes such marques as AC, Ascari, Berkeley, Broadspeed, Chevron, Evante, Gilbern, Ginetta, Gordon-Keeble, Lotus, Lynx, Marcos, McLaren, Monica, Ogle, Lotus, GSM, GTD, Lenham, Lister, Panther, Piper, Reliant, Trident, TVR, WSM etc. Over 300 models in total, each one described and illustrated. *Planned publication date: November 1997.*

Volume 4 – Sequel to volume 2, this is another comprehensive buyer's guide, this time covering every kit car produced between 1985 and the present day. Well over 500 different models detailed and illustrated, each with an information panel including price guide. *Planned publication date: September 1998.*

Other titles available from Bluestream Books and of special interest to the kit car enthusiast include:

THREE-WHEELERS – The complete story of trikes from 1885 through to the present day, including chapters on the first three-wheelers, Morgan, bubblecars and microcars, Reliant, 1970s fun cars, Lomax, 1980s & '90s kit cars and concept machines. 168 pages, over 400 photographs and highly entertaining.

COBRA REPLICAS – A book devoted to the current crop of thunderous, monster sports cars built to recreate the sensational AC Cobra of the 1960s. Includes the Hawk, Dax Tojeiro, Unique Autocraft Python, GD427, Ram, Magnum, BRA 289, Southern Roadcraft, Crendon 427, Pilgrim and Cobretti. 120 pages, lots of great photographs.

PERFORMANCE ROADSTERS – An in-depth look at the hugely popular market for Seven-esque sports cars of light weight, functional design and exhilarating performance. Long chapters on the Caterham Seven, Westfield SE, SEi & V8, Tiger Super Six, Dax Rush, Sylva Striker, Robin Hood and Vindicator, each one including history, factory and model details. 158 pages, generously illustrated.

THE WHICH KIT? GUIDE – This annually updated publication provides a comprehensive introduction to the best models offered by the kit car industry. All the major manufacturers' cars are fully described, including details of the company background, donor cars required, kit contents, budget on-road costs, current addresses, brochure prices and 'phone numbers. Over 100 different models detailed. 148 pages, 80 of them in colour, lots of superb photographs.

KIT CAR BUILDING – Dealing with everything from initial factory visits, cost estimating and choosing your kit, from donor parts preparation and general planning to rolling chassis assembly, through electrical systems and interior trimming to final detailing and on to law and registration, this is the ultimate reference work for anyone planning to build a kit car. 176 pages, 450 photographs and illustrations.

For further details and prices of these books, or to order by credit card, contact the publisher:

Bluestream Books, 1 Howard Road, Reigate, Surrey RH2 7JE
Tel: 01737 222030 Fax: 01737 240185

About the Author...

Chris Rees is an experienced motoring journalist and author who began his career writing about strange cars and kits and has never managed to shake off the affliction. He worked on *Kit Car* magazine during its formative years in the early 1980s and has since contributed to many classic and specialist car magazines, including *Which Kit?*, the UK's leading kit car title.

Chris has written a number of motoring books, including *British Specialist Cars, Microcar Mania* and, for this publisher, *Three-Wheelers*. He's a real enthusiast for driving oddball cars and many of the machines described in *Classic Kit Cars* have passed through his hands. He lives in Berkshire with wife Gabriella and three kids.

And about the Editor...

Little did Peter Filby realise, as he wrote his first monthly feature on kit cars for *Car* magazine in 1972, how drastically he was about to change the course of his life. At the time there was a clear need for some unfortunate motoring journalist to bring Britain's fascinating and innovative specialist kit car industry to a wider public, and Peter rather fell into the job. He was soon writing regularly for magazines such as *Autocar, Motor, Hot Car* and *Auto Enthusiast*.

Peter turned to publishing his own magazine in 1979. The success of *Alternative Cars* led in 1981 to a second title, *Kit Cars & Specials*, which soon evolved into *Kit Car*. In 1987 he launched *Which Kit?*, which today is well respected as the country's best and most authoritative kit car magazine. Other activities include book publishing, kit car show organising and, of course, driving. Peter has owned many of the models featured in *Classic Kit Cars*, including a Unipower GT, Maya GT, Heron Europa, Viking Minisport, Trident Venturer, Jago Samuri, Magenta LSR, MFE Magic, JBA Javelin, Lomax 223, Marlin Berlinetta and Opus HRF.

Which KIT?

UNQUESTIONABLY BRITAIN'S LEADING KIT CAR MAGAZINE

At least 100 *pages every month*

- Full road tests
- Detailed kit build-ups
- In-depth technical features
- Readers' cars
- Latest models
- All the latest news
- Fascinating historical features
- Club news
- Loads of classified ads
- Competitions

*Available at all good newsagents or on a terrific added-value annual subscription at £35 (£48 in EU countries) for which you get **Two Free Extra Publications & Several Special Offers On Reduced Price Books.** Cheques, postal orders and credit card orders accepted. Details from **Blueprint Books Ltd**, 1 Howard Rd, Reigate, Surrey RH2 7JE Tel: 01737 225565 Fax: 01737 240185*